ESSENTIAL
JEET KUNE DO

By TIM TACKETT

Library of Congress Cataloging-in-Publication Data:

Name(s): Tackett, Tim -- author.
Title: Essential Jeet Kune Do / by Tim Tackett.

Description: Los Angeles, California : Empire Books, 2019.
Description based on print version record and CIP data provided by publisher; resource not viewed.

Identifiers: LCCN 2017048819 (print) | LCCN 2017050680 (ebook) | ISBN 9781949753080 (ebook) | ISBN 9781949753080 (pbk.)

Subjects: LCSH: Martial Arts -- Techniques. | Martial Arts -- Techniques.

Classification: LCC GV1114.3 (ebook) | LCC GV1114.3 .F7155 2017 (print) DDC 796.8--dc23.

LC record available at https://lccn.loc.gov/2017048818

DEDICATION

THIS BOOK *is*
Dedicated to Our Grandchildren:

Aaron Medina

Brandon Medina

Jacob Tackett

Caleb Tackett

Courtney Medina

Delaney Medina

and

Aleah Tackett

ACKNOWLEDGEMENTS

I WANT TO THANK the students and
instructors who posed for the photographs
included within this book:

Dennis Blue

Jeremy Lynch

Mark Buster

Paul Kim

and

Jacob Tackett

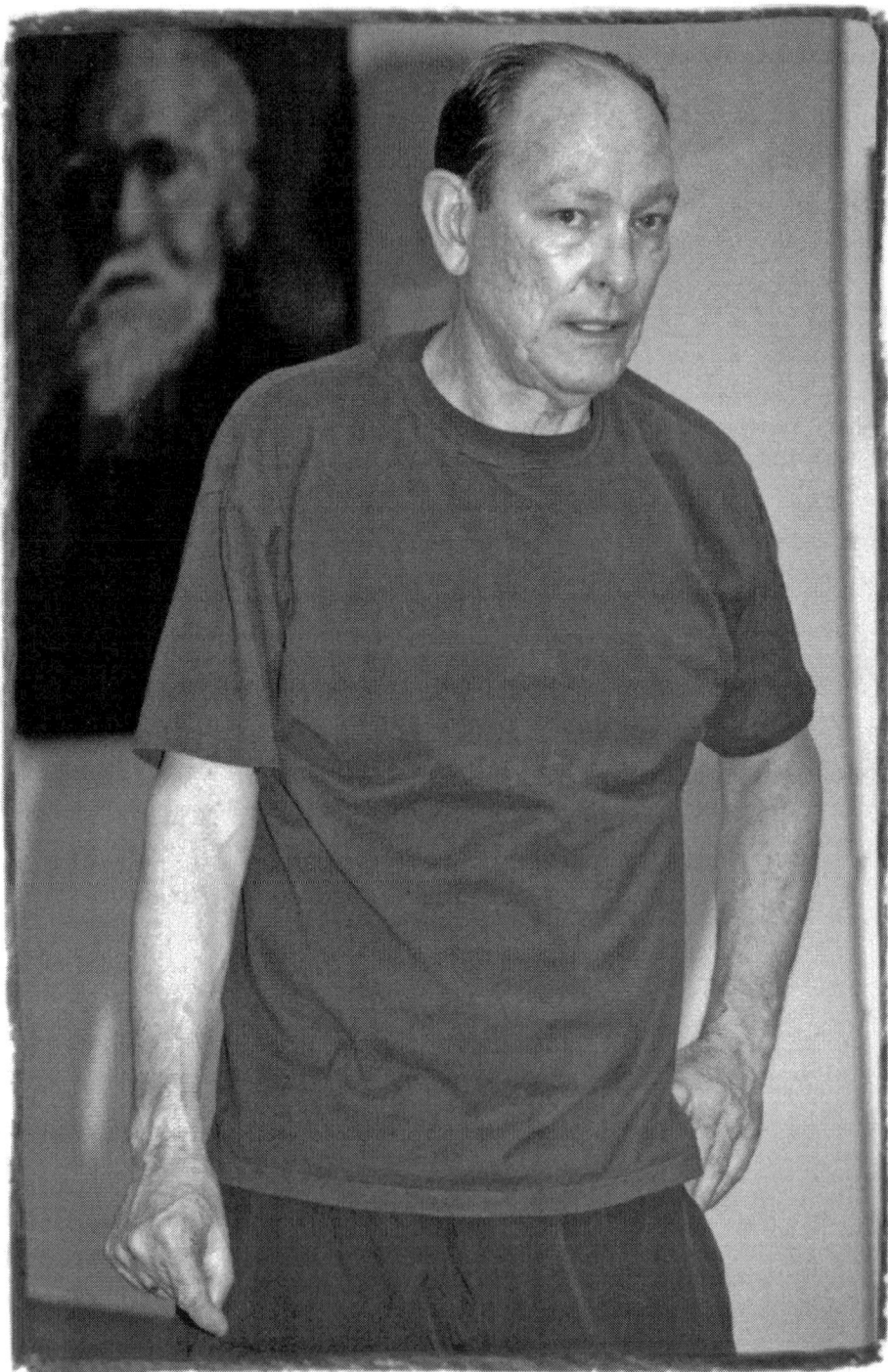

PREFACE

My Martial Art Journey

TO UNDERSTAND WHERE I AM NOW in my martial art journey, you need to know where it all started. I was raised in Redlands, California. From the time I was in grade school I was interested in martial arts. I bought some books on World War II combatives and would practice from books like *Hands Off*, by W.E. Fairbairn, *Do or Die*, by Anthony Drexel-Biddle, and some others. When I was in junior high school, the Police Chief was Wesley Brown, who wrote *Hand-to-Hand Combat* with a couple of other authors. I was going to school at the time and since I knew his daughter, I was able to get ahold of a copy.

My first official martial art training started in 1953 when a judo instructor started teaching at our local YMCA. Unfortunately he left after about 7 months. It wasn't until I got stationed with U.S Air Force in Taipei Taiwan at the beginning of 1962 that I had a chance to study martial arts again. My wife was teaching at the Taipei American School during the day, and I was working at the Shu Lin Kou Air force Base mostly in the late afternoon and late evening at the recreation center. When I went to visit the gym next door next to the center I met Chen Mei Shou who was working part time at night there. I soon found out that he was a Judo and Kuo Shu teacher. Kuo Shu was what the Chinese called their art. It means National Sport. In the U.S. it was called it kung fu. He invited me to come to his school, which was not too far from where we lived in downtown Taipei. I started training there 6 days a week mostly in Southern Chinese Shaolin and Hsing-i.

One day I went to the main park in Taipei after class and saw an old Chinese man doing what looked like a slow motion dance. I asked what it was that he was doing, and one of his students who spoke English said it was Tai Chi. I also found out that he also taught a different form of hsing-i. I started training with him after I finished working in Chen's gym. The man's name was Yuan Tao. He was a former Nationalist Chinese Army General and was one of the most famous martial teachers in Taiwan. I also met a young man who was doing a very fancy Northern Shaolin form. I started talking to him about what he was doing. He invited me to train with him. His name was Shun Mon Wei. He was the number one student of Han Ching Tang. He was famous mainland chin-na master as well as Northern Chinese Shaolin. Chin-na is called the art of seizing and has locks and throws similar to Jui Jitsu. All of a sudden I found myself studying Kuo Shu 7 hours 6 days a week. My ultimate aim was to learn enough that I could open a Kuo Shu school to help me finish my college education. In September of 1964 my wife, two children and I returned home. We bought a house in my hometown of Redlands. After one year of junior college I started school at the University of California at Riverside. At that time no one really knew what Kuo Shu was or even heard of kung fu. All there was at that time was mostly a few karate schools. I decided to call my school the School of Chinese Karate.

The first martial art school that I visited when I got back from Taiwan was Ed Parker's school in Pasadena. Ed had me show a lot of what I learned in Taiwan. Some of the students there would end up being good friends when I started my JKD training in 1971. After class I went to dinner with Dan Inosanto and Steve Golden. I started taking my students to various karate type tournaments. Every year I took a group of my students to compete in Ed Parker's yearly tournament, and every time I would see and talk with Dan Inosanto as he always helped to run the event. In 1967 I saw Bruce Lee's famous demo there. I was impressed and very interested in learning more about what he was showing, but with college, teaching in my gym, and living 70 miles away from the Chinatown school. It was too difficult.

In 1968 I started graduate work on a 2-year program to get my Master of Fine Arts in Theater Arts. Because I had to do so many of my work nights either acting, directing or working on the crew of plays, there were many nights that I couldn't teach. I then closed my school and rented the local American Legion one night a week. I chose Wednesday. When I was unable to teach that night Bob Chapman, my first student, would teach for me. I finally graduated in 1970 and started teaching drama at Montclair High School.

In 1971, I felt I now had the time to study martial arts again. I was tired of teaching. I just wanted to learn.

I went with Bob Chapman in late 1971 to visit a Tai Chi School in Los Angeles. I stared talking to the Sifu's assistant, Dan Lee. He asked if I had ever heard of Jeet Kune Do. I told him that I had. He asked me if I wanted to learn it. I told him that I did. I'm not sure why, but he gave me Dan Inosanto's unlisted phone number.

When I phoned him, Dan remembered me and invited me to come with Chapman on Tuesday night. When we got there, there were only about 8 students there. That night I got to know Bob Bremer, Dan Lee, Richard Bustillo, Pete Jacobs, Tony Luna, and Jerry Poteet.

Bob Chapman and I started coming every Tuesday, Thursday and many Saturdays. The lessons were in Dan Inosanto's backyard school. It was about a 1-and-1/2 hour drive from my house. After teaching high school all day on Tuesday and Thursday we would drive to the backyard school. Would then probably return home between 12 and 1 a.m. Then get up at 6 to get ready to drive 40 minutes to teach.

In 1974 Dan gave me permission to teach a small non-profit group with no publicity. I stopped renting from the American Legion and moved the class to my garage and have been there ever since. So as not to advertise that we were teaching Jeet Kune Do, we called ourselves "The Wednesday Night Group" So it was in 1974 that I created the Wednesday Night Group.

Over the years a few people showed up, kept coming, and showed us some real world combat skills and a proper attitude towards reality fighting. The first person that showed up was Bert Poe. He had been training as a Marine Raider, but the war ended before he saw combat in World War II. He did see combat in Korea where he was wounded. He had also been a boxer and learned combat techniques in various places around the world. He worked with us on what he called dirty fighting and dirty boxing. He really believed in Bruce Lee's idea of efficiency and taking what is offered you. We added what he showed us to what we teach.

Once he retired from being a crane operator, Bob Bremer started coming by ever Wed night. He had trained a lot privately with Bruce after he closed his Chinatown school. While most of our curriculum comes from what I learned from Dan Inosanto in class as well as privately, Bob showed us some things that he had focused on when working with Bruce. These are all in this book and include:

(1) *The Hammer Principle Drill* to learn to get rid of your preparation and to see your opponent's so you can intercept with confidence;

(2) *The Leg Obstruction,* which we use as our main instrument for both attack and defense;

(3) How to really use the *Straight Lead Punch* to intercept;

(4) More efficient *Trapping;*

(5) How to throw the *JKD Back Fist;* and,

(6) How to look at what works, what doesn't, when it works and against what opponent, and show you how to take what is offered you.

Between Bob and Bert we started to really analyze what we were doing and started throwing out techniques that left too many openings or were not efficient enough. Bob explained that Bruce told him that a

JKD man must be like a sculptor not a painter in that he should learn to take away instead of adding. He said why do you need 20 responses for a single stimuli? Between Bob and Bert we started coming up our essence of Jeet Kune Do. We'll share some of what Bert taught us later in this book. The last to show up was a friend of Bob's named Sonny Bygum. Sonny was a Vietnam Vet and had been a Navy UDT man before and after they became the Seals. Sonny had been a long-range iron sight rifle champion, boxer, race driver, bow hunter, and knife maker. He worked with some of us on long range shooting and reality training. All of them and others like Dan Inosanto have given us a roadmap to see the reality of both armed and unarmed combat.

Over the years we seem to have attracted more than a few combat veterans. One example is my first JKD student and senior instructor, Dennis Blue. Dennis is a former Army Special Forces soldier. He was awarded the Silver Star for bravery in a combat mission, and Lloyd Kennedy a great grappling teacher and ex army Ranger and Vietnam veteran. We are still in my garage.

Come by sometime.

The Different Eras in the Evolution of BRUCE LEE'S *Art*

IT MUST BE REMEMBERED that when Bruce Lee came to the U.S. in 1959, he was only 18 years old. His main martial art was Wing Chun. He had studied this art since the age of 13. His first student was Jesse Glover who went to Edison High School in Seattle with him. Through Jesse Bruce started training his second student, Ed Hart. Later he started teaching James Demile and then Taky Kimura. At that time Bruce Lee mainly taught a modified version of Wing Chun with some techniques from other gung fu systems. After about a year, Bruce, tired of being a bus boy at Ruby Chow's restaurant, opened a school with Taky as his assistant instructor. In 1962 Bruce started teaching James Lee, Allen Joe, and George Lee. All became great friends and called themselves the Four Musketeers. The last one Allen Joe, passed away early in 2018.

In 1963, Bruce moved his family to Oakland, leaving the Seattle school in Taky Kimura's capable hands. In Oakland Bruce started a process of shedding some of his old techniques and adding some new elements to his personal martial art. He added a major emphasis on physical conditioning. Bruce also added Western boxing footwork to add mobility to his art, and Western boxing punching to add variety and angles to his punching repertoire. At this time Jun Fan Gung Fu, which is what Bruce Lee called his art, consisted of wing chun trapping and straight punches with four corner simultaneous blocking and hitting, a mixture of Northern and Southern Chinese kicking techniques with angle punching and footwork from boxing.

In 1966 Bruce made his move to Los Angeles to co-star in the Green Hornet television show, and left James Lee in charge of the Oakland school. While in Los Angeles, Bruce made many trips to both Oakland and Seattle to work with James and Taky.

In 1967 Bruce opened the Chinatown school with Dan Inosanto as the head instructor. At this time Bruce started adding Western fencing theory to his martial art. His front hand finger jab was used in a similar way to a Western fencing foil. He adapted fencing attacks into the five ways of attack. But most important of all he took from Western fencing the most efficient defensive technique, which is to intercept your opponent's attack with a stop hit. Bruce Lee felt that being able to stop hit is so important that he named his art *Jeet Kune Do*. The name of his art means "The Way of the Intercepting Fist" in English. It is principle of intercepting your opponent's attack that has become the core essence of what he taught.

With all of the above in mind, how should someone from, let's say, the Taky era look at a technique from the Chinatown era which seems to contradict the way Bruce taught them to do it? First of all we must get over the concept of what is right and wrong. It is my opinion that the techniques from all the eras have value and are in their own way correct. We must also keep in mind that the three eras were not totally separate as they flowed from one to another. Having studied with various students of Bruce Lee from the Chinatown era, I can state unequivocally that there are many variances in the way Bruce taught different students in a private setting. A careful study of Bruce's notes from the Chinatown era shows that while he seemed to teach the same things to different people, he made sure they focused on what would be better for their body type. It is clear from working with different Chinatown students that Bruce Lee tailored his instruction to the individual so that they would do what worked best for them. This can be a small difference punching with a diagonal fist instead of a vertical fist, or a large difference as the stop kick with its most common follow-up. He seemed to teach people of smaller stature to do a shin-knee side kick followed by a finger jab. For people of larger stature, like Bob Bremer, for whom it would be more efficient to crash the line, he taught a leg obstruction followed by a snapping diagonal punch. In the above case neither technique is right or wrong. They're just different.

One thing I know for sure is that Bruce Lee was not looking for an inferior way to do something. The idea that a technique from the Chinatown era is inferior to a technique from an earlier era would be opposite of all we know about Bruce Lee. After all he was audacious enough to write in a magazine article an invitation to anyone reading it to drop by the Chinatown school and full contact spar. Bob Bremer told me that more than one person showed up to spar, watched the training for a while, then changed their mind and left.

One example of a change between Bruce Lee's first era and the Chinatown school is the straight blast. Bruce told Bob Bremer that there are really two straight blasts. He told Bob to use the wing chun shoulder square blast when your opponent is right in your face to get him off of you and stun him. This gives you the proper distance for the one-inch penetration-snapping punch. Once you get the proper distance you finish your opponent off with a straight blast that uses the weight of your body by throwing your shoulders into the punches as well as your entire body. This is what Bruce lee would call a non-crispy attack which can also use boxing hook punches as well as straight line punches. But this should only be used after your opponent is injured and would be unable to counter attack effectively. An example of this can be seen in a video taken in Bruce Lee's backyard where his is punching the heavy bag with heavy hooks. He, of course would never have attacked someone with this method unless it was safe to do so. If you want to see this type of straight blast in action look at Jack Dempsey attacking Jess Willard in their title fight. I know Bruce Lee watched it.

I feel that all of Bruce Lee's students should make an effort to learn as much as possible, or at least experience, the techniques and drills of all the phases of Bruce Lee's martial arts. We should try to understand why Bruce threw away what he did; why he changed certain things; why he added certain things. We need to know, for example, if his not focusing on the wooden dummy in Chinatown was because he had already got the value out of it, or if he found a training method that he felt was more productive. We can't know, only guess.

If by some miracle Bruce Lee could come back for a short visit, I would ask him, *"Sifu, of all the techniques you learned, of all the drills you did, and of all the exercises you went through, which ones were the most important? Which ones do you feel were a total waste of time? And which ones were essential for turning you into the great martial artist*

you became?" Although we cannot know the answer, I feel that students from all the phases of Bruce Lee's life should get together in the spirit of mutual cooperation and love for the legacy that Bruce Lee left us and try to the best of our ability to answer these questions. I know that we would all become better martial artists and teachers if we could do this.

After all we can't really know what JKD would look like if Bruce Lee were still around to look into the most efficient ways to use the human body for combat. Probably a student of Bruce's would look at what we were doing in 1973 and say that it looks as if we had different teachers. What we need to do is look at the core curriculum and use it as a guide into our own investigation into the most efficient way to use the human body for combat. I feel that by sticking to Bruce Lee's principles of combat while at the same time learning and developing our own JKD we will honor Bruce's memory in a way that he would approve of.

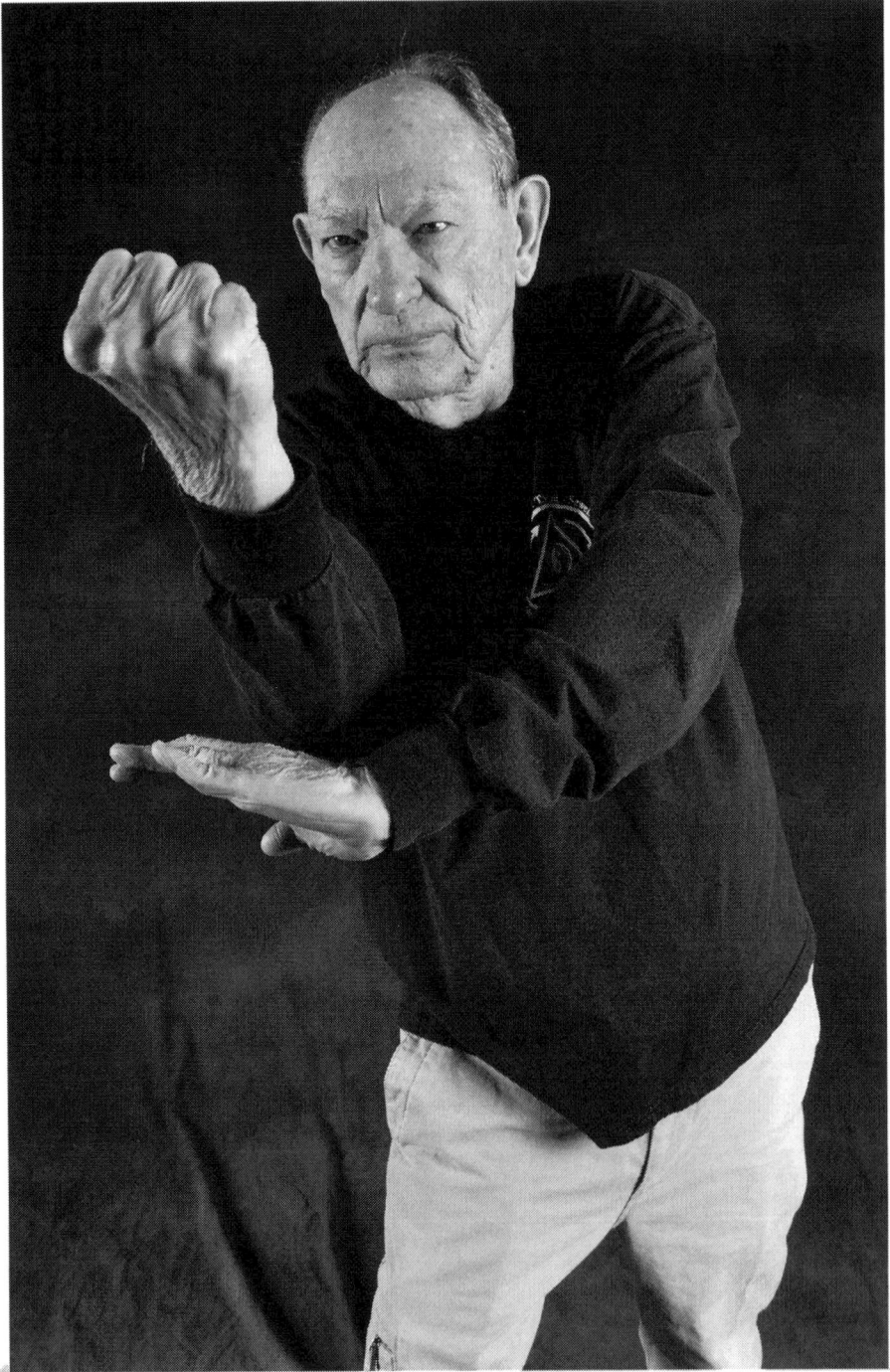

INTRODUCTION

What *is* ESSENTIAL JEET KUNE DO?

TO REALLY BE ABLE TO DO a martial art technique efficiently and without thought you will need to practice it thousands of times. Since to do that with all the techniques in this book would be impossible, this book will serve as a way to decide what will work the best for you and what aspects of JKD you need to keep, as well as throw away. I feel that it would be impossible to learn this from your instructor, as he will mainly focus on what works best for him. I have been fortunate to have learned from many of the senior students of Bruce Lee and have noticed that they all focus on certain things and not on what some the others are doing. For some it may be the boxing aspects. For some it may be footwork. For others it was trapping energy and the Wing Chun elements. It was only when we started focusing on the Western fencing aspects of JKD that I was able to understand and focus on what has become my essential tools in JKD. Of course, an instructor cannot just hand you what will become your essence or foundation of your own JKD. This is something that you must discover for yourself as you work to become more a more efficient JKD practitioner.

The purpose of this book is too show you most of what we teach in my garage and the basic principles behind each. Once you have worked on these, you will come to realize what will work for you and what will not. Some of you will want to focus on distance and footwork. Others will feel comfortable crashing the line. Whatever works for you is the main thing. Just use the book as guideline to discover your own essential JKD.

TIM TACKETT

What *is* JEET KUNE DO?

BASICALLY JEET KUNE DO CAN BE DESCRIBED as balanced relaxed and functional structure based mainly on Bruce's unique combination of Western Fencing/Boxing/Wing Chun.

Bruce Lee on Jeet Kune Do:

1. Jeet Kune Do is training and discipline toward the ultimate reality of combat. The ultimate reality is the returning to one's primary freedom, which is simple, direct and non-classical;

2. A good Jeet Kune Do Man does not oppose force with force, or give way completely. He has no technique; he makes his opponent's technique his technique. He has no design; he makes opportunity his design;

3. One should respond to circumstances without artificial and wooden prearrangement. Your action should be like the immediacy in Jeet Kune Do of a shadow adapting to a moving object;

4. In Jeet Kune Do, one does not accumulate but eliminate. It is not daily increase, but daily decrease. The height of cultivation runs to simplicity. It is not how much fixed knowledge one has accumulated; rather it is what one can apply in an alive setting that counts;

5. The truth is outside of all fixed patterns; and,

6. Mainly Jeet Kune Do is a combination of Wing Chun Kung Fu, Western boxing and fencing.

A. THE WING CHUN CONNECTION

The Centerline (explained): The centerline is the straight line running from the center of the top of your head to your groin.

This line includes many of the most vulnerable parts of your body from your throat to your groin. The basic idea is that if you cover that line with your guard, to hit you your opponent must either remove the guard by faking or trapping, or to go around it.

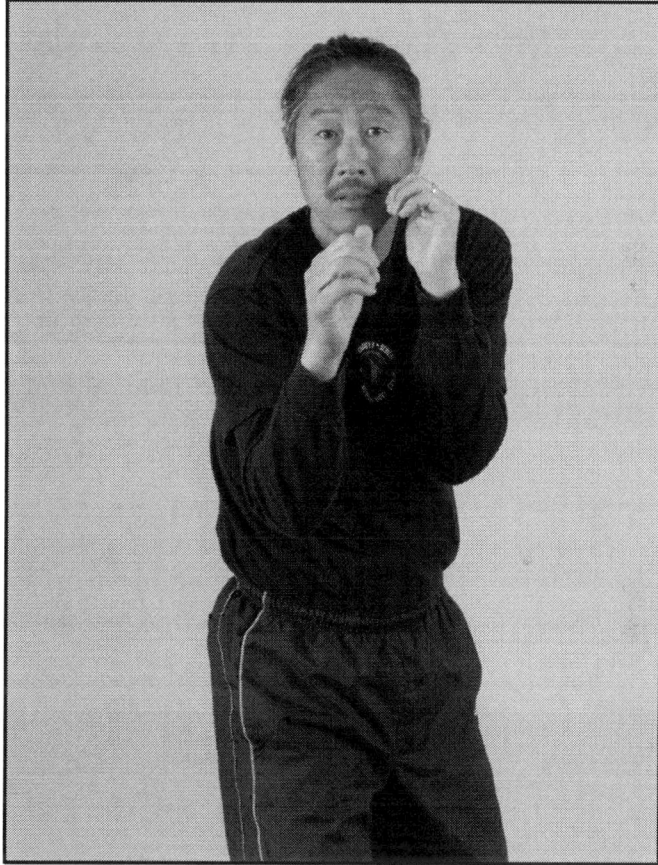

SLIDING LEVERAGE: One of the main Wing Chun self-defense principles is to use your defense against an attack as an offensive strike. This is done, as shown below, by using leverage to counter the attack as you hit.

Outside Sliding Leverage

NAT STANCE BASIC DRILL:

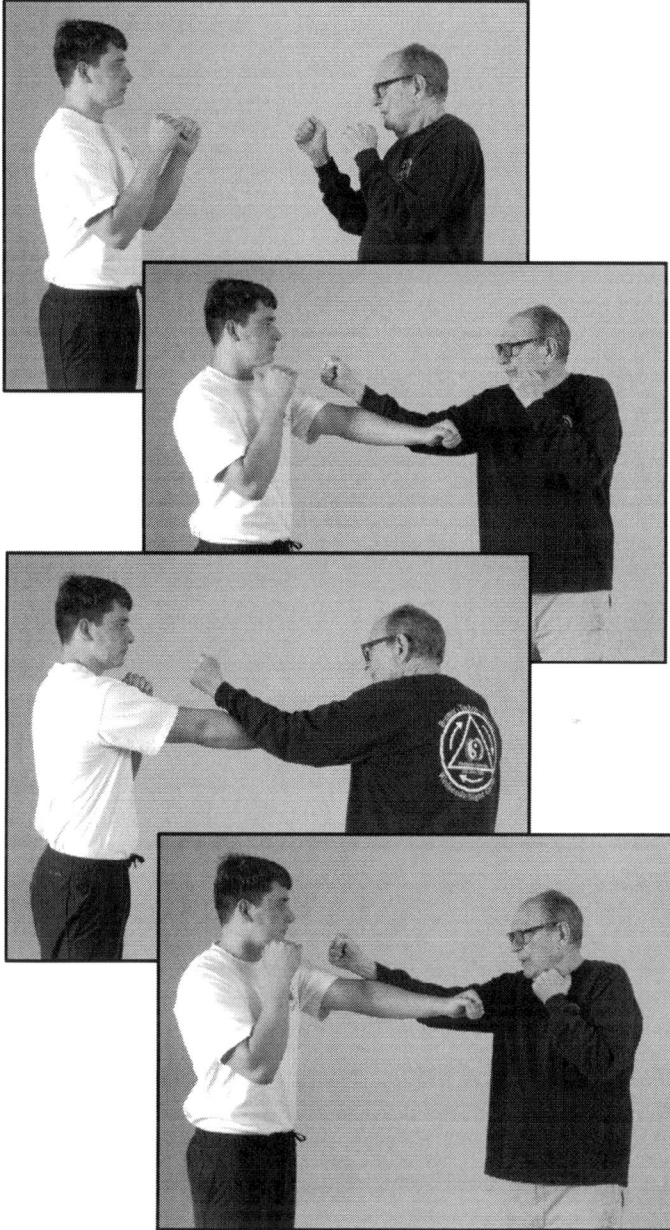

INSIDE SLIDING LEVERAGE: Inside sliding leverage will not work if you try to counter a punch with your shoulder forward as your opponent will have the stronger leverage

Below we show how energy that works outside does not work inside.

RIGHT LEAD AGAINST LEFT LEAD (RTL): The *correct* way -- By keeping your shoulder square and using your elbow for leverage on your finger jab you will stay inside his strike. Try to practice this by not using a parry with your finger jab until you can safely use sliding leverage without any problem. You can then use the cross parry with the finger jab.

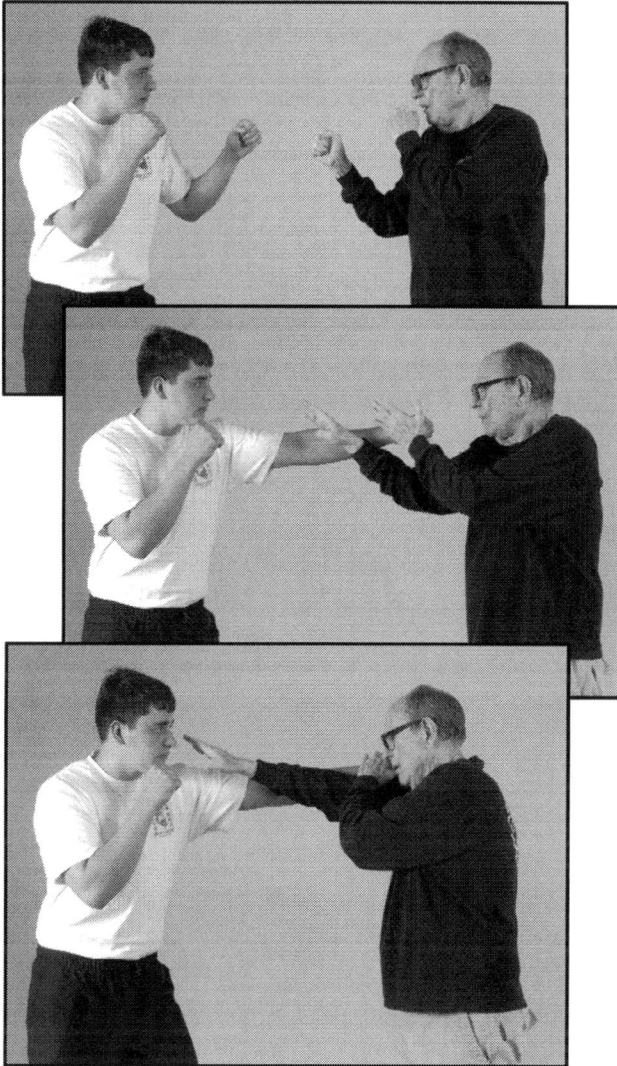

DISENGAGEMENTS: Disengagements are used to go from one line to another. For example, to go from one line that is covered to an open line. This is also a major principle of Western fencing.

(1) *Small Disengagement*: Going from the outside to the inside.

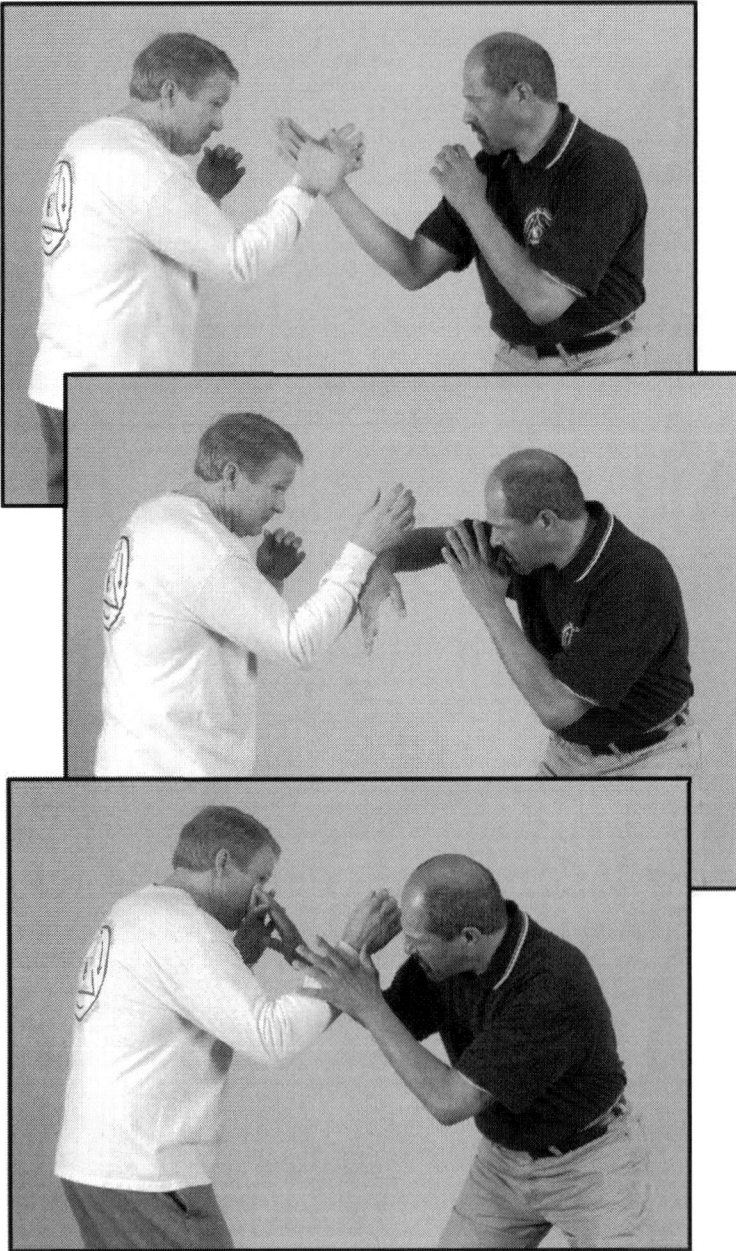

(2) *Large Disengagement*: Going from one outside line to the other with a palm strike.

TRAPPING: (Covered in section on *5 Ways of Attack*)

B. THE BOXING CONNECTION

"Boxing is about being able to hit your opponent while he can't hit you."
--- CUS D'AMATO

(1) Boxing gives us more variety in punches like bent arm punches.

Bent arm punches make possible:
- A. More angles to punch (flexibility without confinement);
- B. More combinations;
- C. Opening opponent's defense; and,
- D. More power and finishing blows.

(2) Efficient Footwork --- As we will see in the section on footwork, fencing and JKD have some similarities.

(3) Full Contact Sparring:
- A. Learning what it is like to be hit and be hit with hard contact punches;
- B. Controlling distance in attack and defense;
- C. Timing in attack and defense;
- D. Learning to roll with a punch; and,
- E. Learning what really works and what does not work in sparring situations.

(4) Basic Boxing Defense --- Shown in detail in section on defense.

(5) Indirect Attacks:
- A. *Feinting and Faking -- Feinting* is the art of using the body in moving to an attack at one point, but then attacking to another line. It involves the footwork, knees, hands, head, eyes, arms, shoulders and trunk.

A *feint* should make your opponent feel "feint." It must look like a real attack.

A *Fake* is an indirect attack will usually occur in two motions: the fake and the hit.

Examples:

In the example below, a low punch is started toward the target (the fake) then the fist is withdrawn and a high backhand hammer fist (the hit) is delivered.

EYE FAKE: Look down to high hit. This look down is exaggerated. You really only need to use your eyes to glance down and quickly hit high *(Sequence beginning at right and shown on next page)*.

FAKE KICK TO PUNCH *(shown below and following page)*

**LOWER BODY
AND FAKE A LOW
BODY PUNCH**

*(Shown at right and
on following page)*

Drop your body one more time as you throw a high rear overhand punch *(Sequence following below)*.

Feint Examples --

RIGHT LEAD AGAINST RIGHT LEAD (RTR): Throw a low punch to a high swinging palm hit all in one motion. *(Photo at right and on following page).*

LOW FRONT HAND PUNCH:
He blocks down with front
hand -- to high rear or trap
and back fist.
*(Sequence beginning at left
and on to following page)*

You should work on combining the above as a drill so you can learn to flow with what is offered you.

Illusive Head and Body Movement

EXAMPLES:

(1) Slipping In and Out Against a Jab or Straight Lead.

A. INSIDE SLIP:

B. OUTSIDE SLIP:

B. OUTSIDE SLIP – TO LOW STRAIGHT LEAD:

C. Inside Slip to High Straight Rear Punch.

(2) Bob and Weave

(3) Snap Back

Infighting – Sometimes you are not able to keep the fighting measure (The fight measure is the safe distance between you and your opponent. The fighting measure is explained in detail below in the section on Western fencing tools) and stay out of the range of your opponent's offensive tools. In that case, you need to have the ability to slip inside his guard and be able to take him out by slipping his punch and take him out with a series of body blows. Boxing is one of the best arts to learn how to do this.

Conditioning – You need to be in great condition to be able to train hard enough to survive in the ring, as well as a street fight.

C. THE FENCING CONNECTION

To be able to intercept an attack before it can get to you, you need to be able to control the distance between you and your opponent. The fight measure is the distance between you and your opponent, so as to be able to touch you with an attack he will have to step forward with his front foot to gain the proper distance. The fighting measure is crucial in fencing. If your opponent is close enough with a fencing foil to be able to hit you without have to move forward, it is almost imposable to be able to react in time to parry the attack. If you can keep your opponent at a distance where to be able to make contact with a punch or a kick, he will have to step forward will give you the time to react and be able parry or intercept the attack.

(1) Intercepting -- The key to Jeet Kune Do is being able to intercept an opponent's attack with a stop hit or kick with enough power to nip the attack in the bud.

> BRUCE: *"Sock it --- everything is there, as soon as the opening is there. When your opponent attacks he will have to leave an opening. At a minimum 1/3 of his body will be open.*
>
> *"When the opponent advances, one intercepts. This is to 'stop the enemy at the gate.'*
>
> *"To reach me, you must move to me. Your preparation of attack offers me a directional commitment to intercept you."*

(2) Footwork -- Footwork training is essential to both maintain the fighting measure as well as allowing you to bridge the gap between you and opponent and attack.

A. LEAD STEP:

The lead step is a quick step forward with the front foot to get in range of the enemy and hit him with a front hand attack. When throwing a lead step hand attack, start with the hand going first then pushing hard with your rear foot as you step forward. Make sure that you to not step too far and be off balance. You should be able to quickly step forward and quickly back if need be.

B. Push Step:

To move forward further than with a lead step, push off with your rear foot as you step forward with your front foot. You then slide up with your rear foot, keeping the same distance as before the push step. To go back, simply push back with the front foot.

C. Quick Advance *(Step & Step)* **with Partner:**

To work on moving forward with fast short steps, one student moves forward by stepping forward by quickly stepping with the front foot followed by a quick step forward with your rear foot. The other student mirrors this footwork by stepping back then moving forward. Practice this by both partners move forward and back keeping the same fighting measure distance.

D. THE STEP AND SLIDE:
You can also move forward and back by stepping forward with
the front while sliding forward with the back foot. To move
back the rear foot will step back while the front foot slides back.
The step and step is great for keeping a safe distance, while the
step and slide is better to attack or to intercept an attack.

E. SLIDE AND STEP (*with Partner, Forward and Back):*
The slide and step. The student moving forward slides his rear
foot up and then steps forward with his front foot. His partner
does the opposite, and moves forward. They both try to
maintain the fighting measure. How far you slide you foot will
depend on the distance you need to attack or to retreat.

F. STEAL A STEP *(with partner)*:

If you just slide up and try to hit your opponent, chances are that you will be out of range if he slides back.

You can steal a step on an opponent who gives grounds or retreats against your attack. From the fighting measure, take a lead step and feint a hand attack. If he gives ground by moving back, quickly slide your rear foot up and step forward and punch with a straight lead.

G. BROKEN RHYTHM FOOTWORK:

Slide back to quick push forward. If your opponent attempts to hit you with hand attack, slide and step back, pushing forward as soon as your rear foot touches the ground. If you do this fast enough, you will have broken his attacking rhythm, as you will be able stop him before he can strike you with another hit.

(3) The beat as a Parry and Hit (Touch and Go)

If your opponent tries to hit you with a jab, you can pat his hand down with a beat parry and hit.

FROM **RTR** --- *Beat (Like a Slap), Parry and Hit*:

FROM LTR AGAINST REAR PUNCH --
Beat, Parry and Hit:

A beat parry is also easy to do against any straight hand attack and at the same kick as you make contact with his hand. It is usually more efficient to use sliding leverage against a straight punch, so that your block is an attack.

SLIDING LEVERAGE AGAINST A STRAIGHT *LEAD* PUNCH:

SLIDING LEVERAGE AGAINST A STRAIGHT *REAR* PUNCH:

(4) Offensive/Defense (Stop Hits)

In JKD your offense is your best defense. If you can maintain the fighting measure between you and any possible opponent, with practice you should be able to intercept any attack with either a stop hit or kick. When in public you should always be aware of anyone who could pose a threat and keep a safe distance between you.

A. ATTACK ON INTENTION:
If you practice the hammer principle long enough, you may be able to feel your opponent's intention to attack you and strike first. Of course, this will depend where you are and who is around, as you never want to be seen as the aggressor.

B. ATTACK ON PREPARATION:
Most of the time there will be some preparation when your opponent attacks. Most common is his step forward to get in range with his attack when at the fighting measure. *(Some common examples are shown on following page.)*

ON HIS PULLING HAND BACK:

Dropping His Shoulder *(Exaggerated to show the opening):*

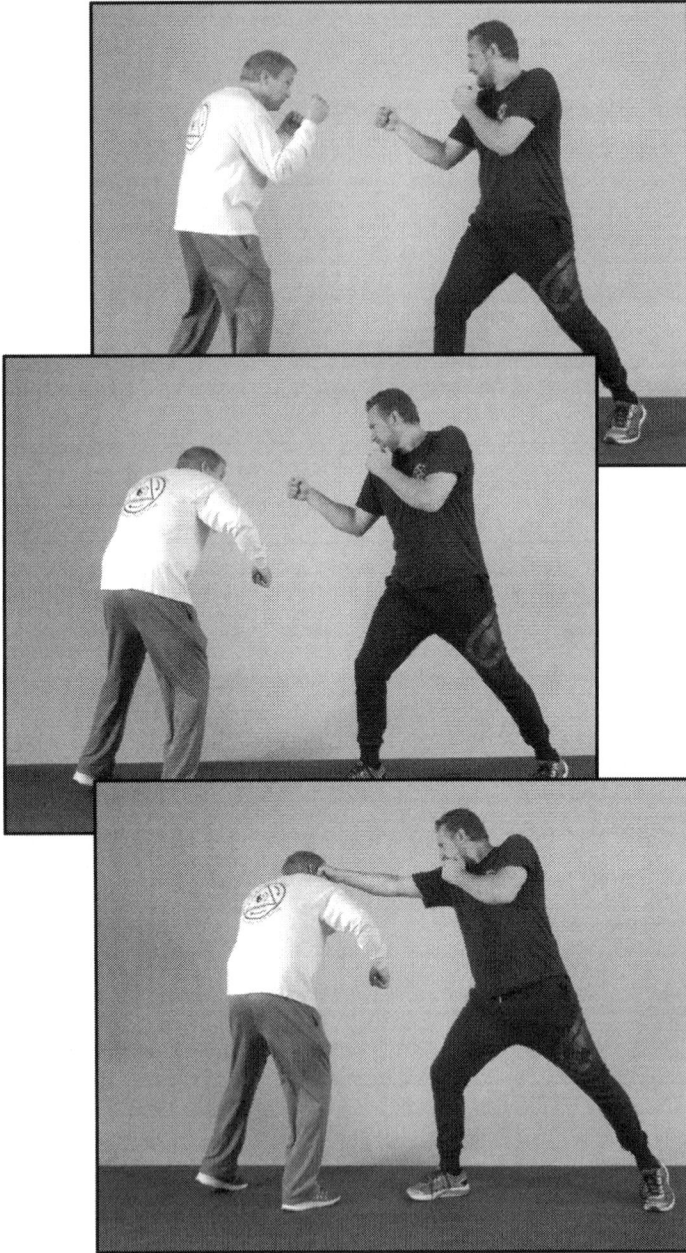

C. ATTACK ON DELIVERY:

When your opponent throws, for example, a straight lead, the time the punch is initiated until it reaches its full extension is one complete beat of time. If you intercept the attack before it has a chance to be completed is called attack on delivery, or on the ½ beat.

ON THE ½ BEAT:

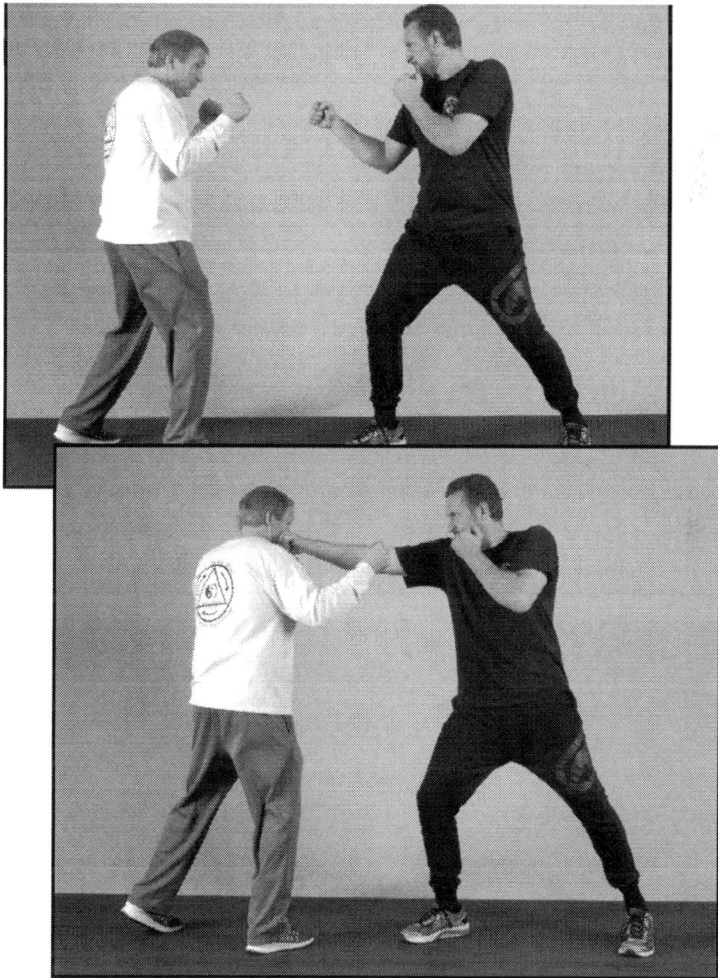

D. ATTACK ON COMPLETION:

To intercept the attack when it has completed its forward movement is call an *attack on completion*. In western fencing, it is called a *time hit*.

E. ATTACK ON RECOVERY:

If you strike your opponent as soon his attack is withdrawn to either return to an on-guard stance or follow up with another attack is called an attack on recovery.

(5) Attacks:

A. BROKEN TIME ATTACK *(Delayed Hit):*

If you start your attack and pause ½ way to completion so that the opponent parries, then renew the attack, you will have "deceived the parry" and scored.

You Hit -- He Parries (shown in following sequence)

You Hit and Stop -- He Over-Parries – You Hit
(shown in following sequence)

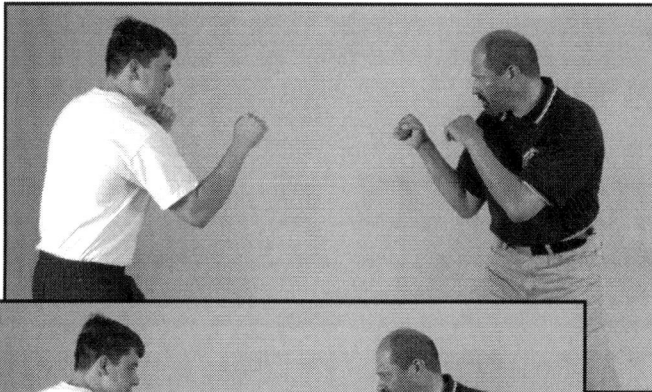

B. FEINTING + DISENGAGEMENT

Feinting to Hit -- *You can feint to open a line, then score a hit.*

LOW TO HIGH

Low to High with Back Fist

HIGH TO LOW

Feinting to Disengagement and Hit -- *These are basically the same disengagements as those found in Wing Chun.*

A. OUTSIDE TO INSIDE

(6) The Hammer Principle:

To do the hammer principle your drop your hand from the elbow only, as if you were hammering in a nail on a wall and then hit as the arm is dropping.

WITH STICK:

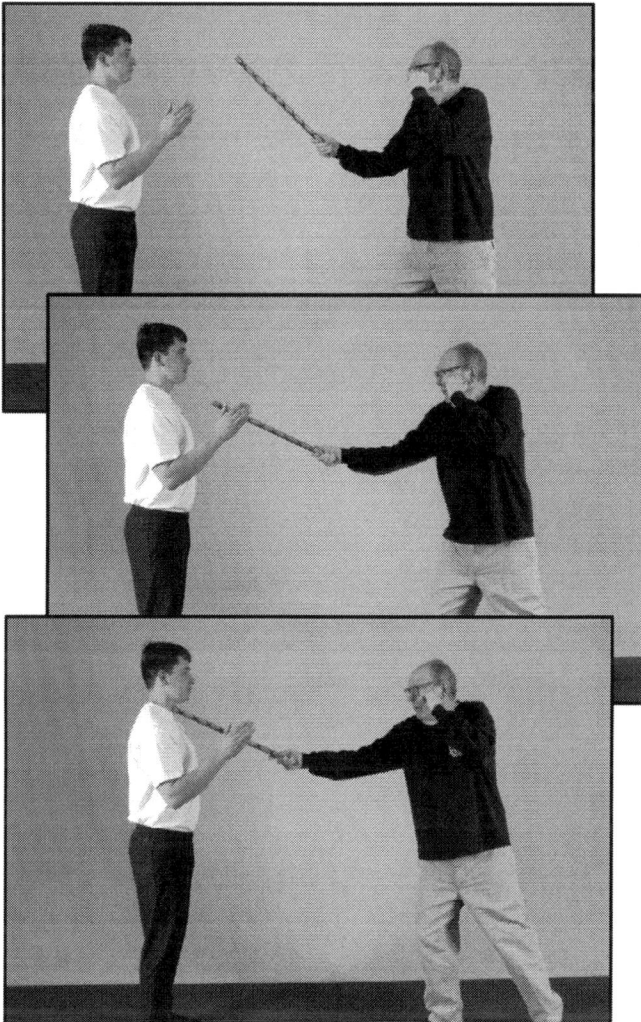

WITH EMPTY HANDS:

Do first with no step. Then do it with a lead step. Then do it with a push step.

When you drop your arm with a hammer like movement, you are doing a non-threatening movement, while your fist has moved closer to the target giving you an advantage in the time of your attack.

Make sure that when you are in an on-guard stance that your fist lines up in a direct line to your opponent's nose and not pointing any higher. If it is too high your opponent will see the drop too easily and you will lose the element of surprise in the attack.

When dropping the hammer, you should not drop it lower than his chin as you thrust your arm forward. When the hand thrusts forward you will create a slight blind spot for a split second

D. THE KUNG FU CONNECTION

Some people claim that JKD is made up of 26 arts, mostly from kung fu arts. I think the confusion comes from a list that Dan Inosanto got from Sifu Lee. It was a list of 26 arts. When I asked Sifu Dan about the list, he told me that Bruce had listed the 26 arts that he had looked into to see how they entered, and if he had a method to counter them. As far as I can tell, the techniques below are the only ones I know that came directly from other arts except from those he took from boxing, fencing, and a few kicks from other arts.

(1) Choi Li Fut

LOW PUNCH TO BACK FIST

(2) Praying Mantis

INVERTED HOOK KICK – RTL

Chapter 1

Basic Principles

1. *Strong Hand Forward:*

Primary use of lead hand/lead leg with coordinated side forward –with knock out power with front hand. With the strong hand forward your main weapon, the straight lead punch, is closer to the target, while your weaker rear hand is farther away so it can gain power as it has farther to travel. To make the strong hand forward work in combat you punch should not be a jab type punch, but rather a full power committed punch. You front hand straight lead should have the same power as when your strong hand is your rear hand and you are throwing a straight rear punch. This will require a lot of work to be able to use it to intercept your opponent's attack with enough power to finish the fight .

BRUCE: *"The best way to win the fight is to just knock him out."*

2. *Take What is Offered You:*

When someone moves into range to attack he will give you an opening so that you can intercept his attack.

EXAMPLES:

ON HIS SHOOT – EYES:
Upward Poe to eyes using the tips of your fingers.

You can also do this by stepping back with your front foot if he gets too close.

On his straight lead – shin/knee side kick

RTL on his Thai style kick – RT step to straight rear)

3. It is important to understand what you are offering or leaving as an opening for your opponent to take advantage of, when you are learning a new technique. Realize what you are you leaving open for his counterattack. A lot of the techniques you will learn are based on attacking or countering a specific attack or style. Also a lot of things work when the opponent in front of you is no good, or you are aware type of opponent you're are facing. When we started putting a worthwhile opponent like a good grappler or a JKD man, who will intercept your attack in front us, our approach to martial arts changed. What good will it do to fake a high hand attack against a grappler who will shoot under it? What good would it do to do the same thing against a JKDer who will stop kick you? When you are learning a new technique, ask yourself, if this would work in street against a real opponent, and you have no idea of what he might do. Start by asking what are you offering him?

4. Try to use the principle of the closest weapon to the nearest target by taking your closest shot for efficiency. Try to use the closest weapon to the nearest target, as it will be the most likely one to score a hit. *RTR*

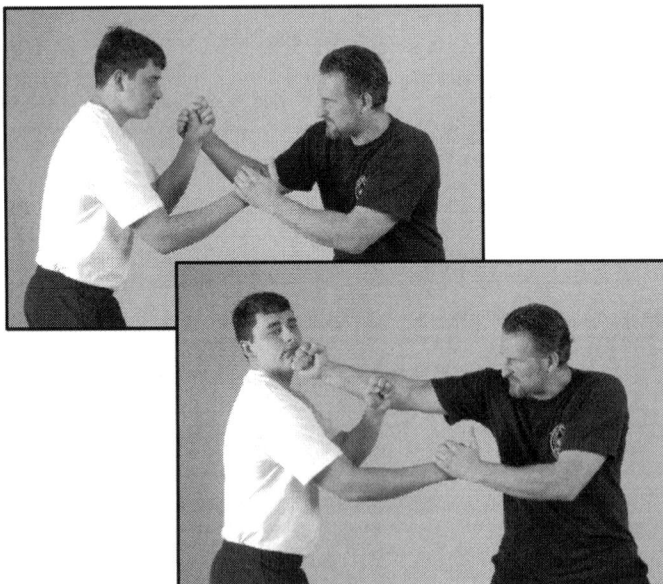

LTR

5. Simplify:

When somebody throws something at you, you simply catch it without thought. Learn to react naturally. For example, if you are taken by surprise something that something like a ball is thrown at your head, you simply duck your head without thought. You responses to different stimuli must be natural and simple.

6. Time Commitment Theory Explained:

When you use one of your tools like a punch or a kick you will be committing a certain amount of time from the moment you start a blow, to either returning to your guard position, or to renew the attack with another strike. The two main ways to deliver a blow to get power is with a snap at the end the blow like the hook kick which when done properly ends like cracking of a whip, or a heavy blow that uses the weight of the hit that goes through the target.

The whipping hook kick is one example of a snappy or crispy attack. The same effect is the waterhose principle done with a side kick. This type of snappy blow is explained in the chapter on kicking. The advantage of a crispy attack is that it can be done so fast that you are committing a minimum amount of time.

The uncrispy or heavy attack is just the opposite. Instead of snapping your hit or kick, using a weight of your arm or leg you hit through your target. This means that your recovery will be slower so that your will be committing more time to your attack. All this really means is that your attack usually will be used as a finishing attack after your opponent is dazed. You should never innate a heavy attack unless you are sure that you can land the blow and finish the encounter.

A. CRISPY AND UNCRISPY -- *also called snappy and heavy.*

EXAMPLES:

SNAPPY/CRISPY PUNCH:
This punch is done by shooting forward as fast as you can with a snap at the elbow, and returning back to the on-guard position. So that you snap the punch and not "push" it, the punch should not have more than a 1- to 2-inch penetration.

71

HEAVY/UNCRISPY: This time the punch penetrates thru the target as if it is going to come out through the back of his head.

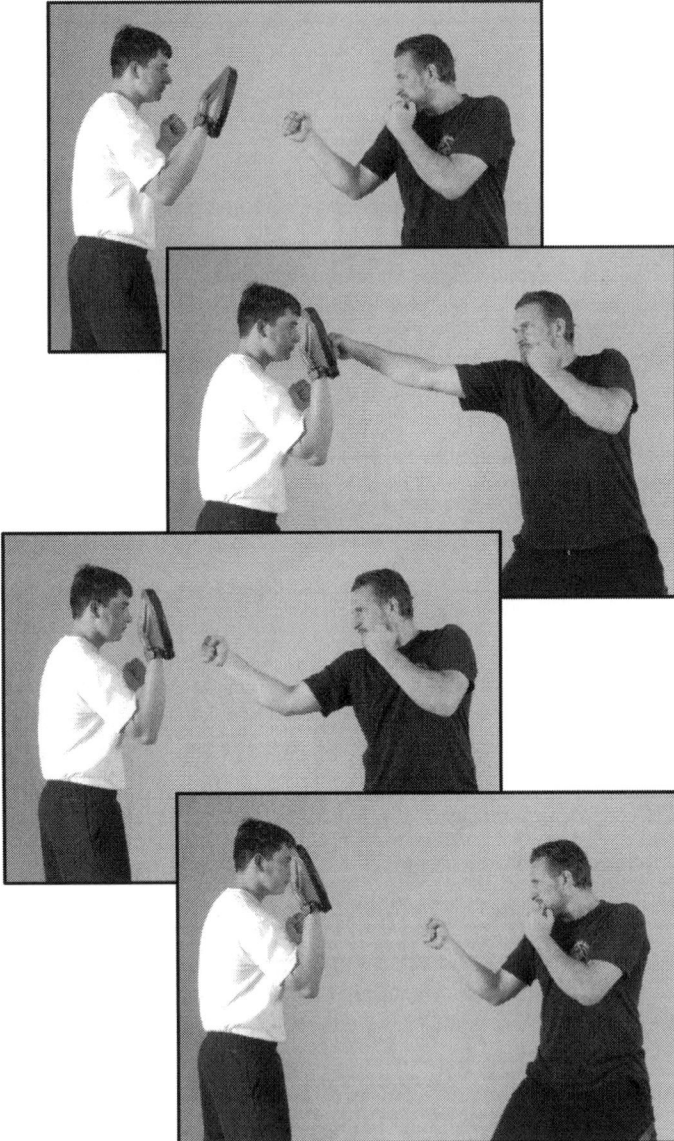

SNAPPY HOOK PUNCH: Throw the punch as you dig the toes of your front foot into the ground. Your punch should snap back to the ready position with no more that a 1- to 2-inch penetration.

Heavy Palm Hit: With the arm as relaxed as possible, swing and smash though the target. Think of your arm as very heavy.

SCOOP KICK: Slide up as you raise your knee a couple of inches past the intended target as you snap the kick, and then pendulum back to the on-guard position

HEEL HOOK KICK: Make sure that you try and kick through the target as you swing your leg.

7. Express Yourself:

BRUCE: *"When one is not expressing himself, he is not free."*

He then struggles by trying to do what is not natural to him, which is the loss of primary freedom. Instead of a loose free movement, the student becomes mechanical and stiff. It is common in traditional martial arts that the student is taught one way to do something so that all the students become clones of the teacher. Unfortunately some of that exists in JKD. I've seen that some of the senior students stress in their teaching what works the best for them. They seem to focus on that aspect when they teach, and their students do the same. This is a natural occurrence, but each student must be given the ability to find out what works the best for himself.

The Jeet Kune Do teacher must expose his students to what he may not do himself, as it may not fit his body type or his personality. A lot of this is not about techniques so much as tactics and strategy. When in sparring or in combat one teacher may focus on footwork and distance for defense, while the other may focus on crashing into his opponent and then controlling him. Others may focus on boxing's midrange tactics. There are sometimes when you may need to do any one of them to survive. It will do you no good to focus on just one way or environment. You must be able to fit into any situation and have honed the necessary tools to do so.

Offensive Defense – No passive moves. A passive move like a block can give your opponent an advantage, as you have done nothing to stop the encounter. No matter how fast you can block and hit you will still leave some time that your opponent can take advantage. This is really apparent it your opponent is faking or feinting with his first hit.

Attitude – Bruce "Sudden (As well as violent) destructiveness." To survive in a street encounter, you must be able to release the tiger inside of you in a controlled manner. Bruce Lee called it emotional content. The advantage of training with equipment like Thai pads and focus gloves is that you can hit them as hard as you can and not injure any training partner. To do this you need to be able to control your hits by staying cool and keep covered and still in total control. Work on visualizing that the focus glove in your mind represents something you hate. Of course, you should not constantly train like that all the time. You will still need to work of things like precision, finesse, and proper technique. Just try and save some time in your training to work on "sudden destructiveness."

Longest Weapon to Closest Target -- One of the most efficient way to attack or counter attack is to use your longest weapon to hit the closest target. It is the opposite the closest weapon to the nearest target.

A. SHIN/KNEE SIDE REAR KICK:
The side rear kick is the longest of kicking tools. To get the maximum distance make sure to roll your hip into it as far as possible.

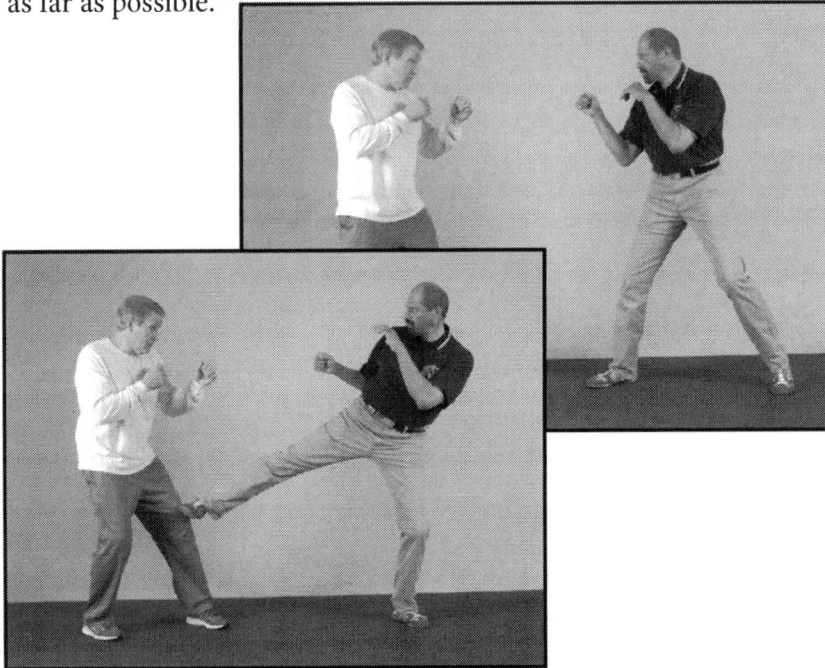

B. FINGER JAB TO EYES

Economy of Motion = Natural Movements --- If someone throws you something, you simply catch it. That's all there is to it. When you throw a straight lead with your elbow out, or bringing the hand back before hitting you are not using the economy of motion. With the elbow out the punch is easier to see and there is no "snap" at the completion of the strike. If you pull your hand back, you are telegraphing the attack. Bath are examples on non-economy of motion.

Generation of power and use of kinetic chain, weight transfer (torque), gravity short arc principle. Explained below in the section on punching.

Refinement of tools --- Best to do a few things well rather than a lot of things not done well. Make sure you can respond to any environment or situation. Be like the sculptor and hack away at what is not necessary.

Make sure you have "a particular medicine for particular disease". For example, if you can defend against most standup attacks but have no defense against someone tries to tackle you, there is a hole in your defensive training.

You need to understand as much as possible about other martial arts or fighters. Bruce had a lot of notes on the strengths and weaknesses of different martial arts on how they entered and defended.

EXAMPLES:

-- The Rusher

-- The Blocker

-- One who uses Distance

Alive Training --- Giving different stimulus to get a different response. (Key to learning how to defend without thought, as there should only be time for the JKDer to respond, as there should be no time to think.)

Daily Decrease --- The 80/20 theory explained: The main idea is not to add and add techniques since no one can learn everything. There is no point to having 20 responses to a single stimulus. It is better to be able to done a few things well than be able to do a lot of things half assed. We try and use the 80/20 theory of training. That is we try to spend 80 % of our time working on what we will use 80% of the time. As I've gotten older, there is now less and less in my toolbox. I think I have boiled my JKD down to its essence.

Learn to hurt him with a flick --- Hit like you are snapping a wet towel.

Here we are using the finger fan as an example:

Chapter 2

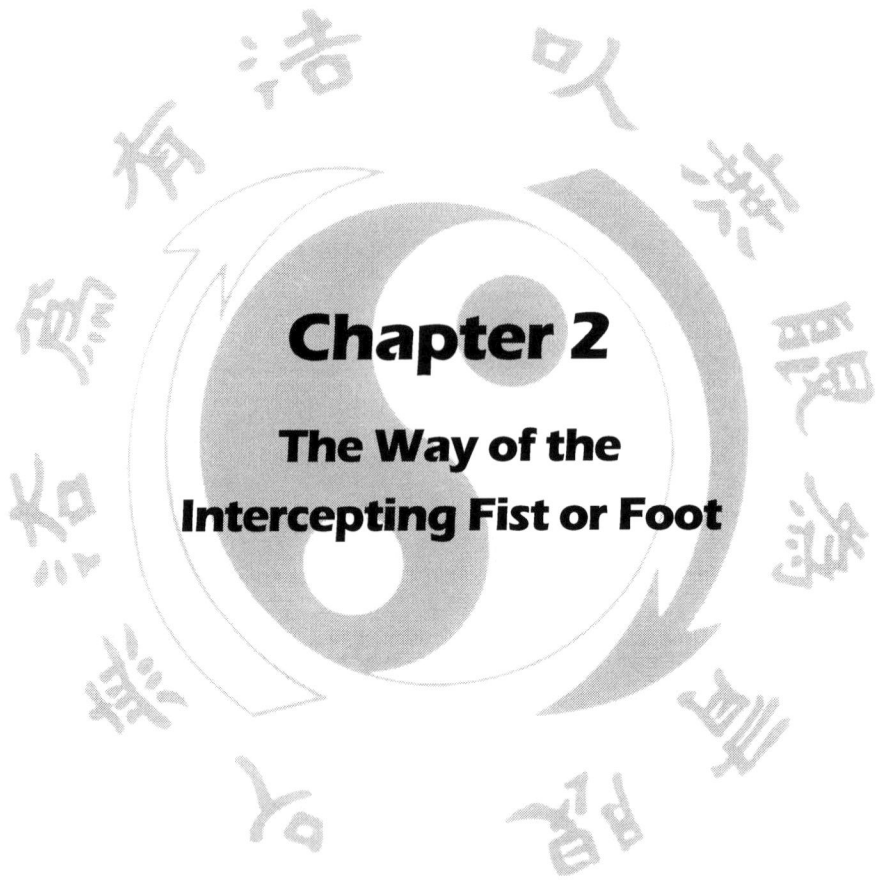

The Way of the
Intercepting Fist or Foot

JEET KUNE DO means the way of the intercepting fist or foot. The safest way to deal with your opponent's attack is to beat him to the punch. In a way JKD is a very moral art as you are merely responding to an attack. The safest way to do that is to enough distance between to give you time to react. This distance comes from Western fencing and is called the fighting measure and will give you the time to react.

If you are at the fighting measure, unless your opponent has a weapon that can be fired or thrown at you, he will need to take a step towards you to make contact with you, giving you time to intercept you. You must be careful to leave just enough distance. Too much distance and your opponent may gather too much momentum and overpower you. Too little distance and you will not have the time to react.

Both at the fighting in a ready stance 1 with his hand fully extended like the end of a finger jab just missing:

This may look like a safe distance and that your opponent needs to take a step forward, but it will not be if your opponent twists his rear foot and transfers his weight to his front leg like the straight lead finger jab. You should only do this to intercept. Because you have so much weight on your front leg and it takes more time commitment, never attack with this hit.

CLOSE UP OF FOOT TWIST:

SHOW WITH STICKS --- *with no twist:*

SHOW WITH STICKS AND WITH FOOT TWIST:

By using the foot twist the thrust is just misses you without having to lean away. This is the secret to making a stop-hit work, as you should be hit just before any parry or block you add. "Just hit!"

When your opponent advancing towards you, he offers you his "advanced target" of his front shin or knee.

Stance and Footwork:

At the most only 2 stances. Not like my kung fu where I learned many stances. It is better to have one basic structure.

STRUCTURE – Everything must work from one structure. I try not to add anything that I have to change my structure to make it work.

READY STANCE: It's not a good idea to jump into one in the street confrontation. For one thing it gives a possible opponent too much information. Very few street thugs will be intimated by your kung fu or karate stance. Let the fact that you are trained be a surprise. That said here is an example of a ready stance at the fighting measure.

From this stance you can intercept with:

SIDE REAR KICK -- by popping down with your rear foot.

SIMPLE LEG LIFT ~~by~~ hopping forward

THE LEG OBSTRUCTION -- with a slight hop forward, if you have the time.

We feel that in a street confrontation to be in a non-threating natural stance with RT foot forward and opponent just simply facing you. If he attacks for example with attacking with a sucker punch, you will be able to defend with leg obstruction as it is easy to do from a natural stance and very efficient.

The leg obstruction is done stationary by popping down with your rear foot.

THE LEG OBSTRUCTION -- *used against a sucker punch.*

Chapter 3

Hand Attacks

BRUCE LEE told Bob Bremer that a JKDer should have sledge-hammers in both hands.

To get the maximum in a snappy punch it should end with a snap 1 to 2 inches beyond the target. You punch through the opponent, yet end with a snap so that there is less chance of damaging the hand.

THE STRAIGHT LEAD PUNCH – Snappy, 1-inch penetration with the main target being the nose.

The fist should not be clenched until impact.

The fist is not vertical for the straight lead. While a vertical hit is very good for any sliding leverage punches, as you can keep you elbow down to get proper leverage and is used for any close range Wing Chun punch, we've found that a punch with the fist at a 45 degree angle --- a 1 to 2 inch penetration with a snap at the elbow is --- the most efficient way to do a straight lead punch.

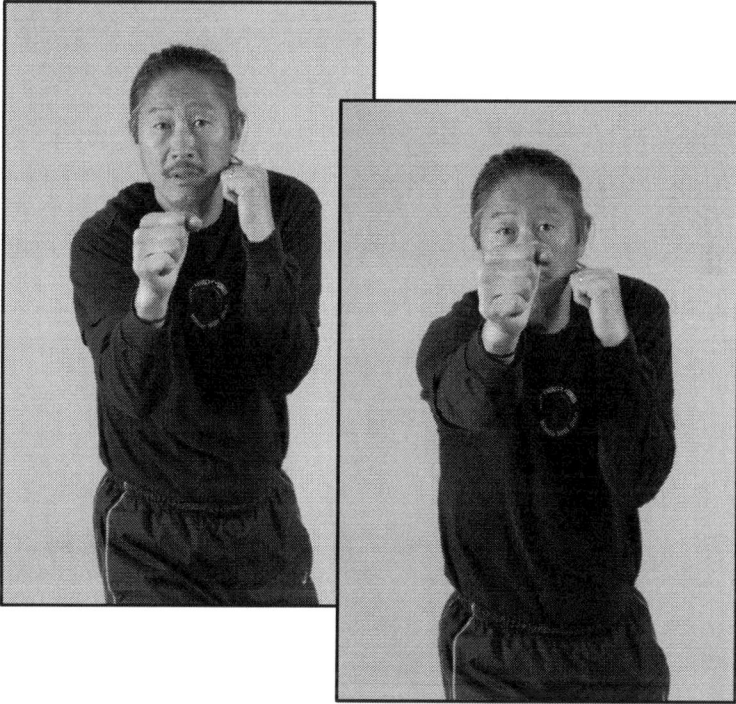

The fist should be at 45 degrees --- This makes the middle knuckles the primary striking surface instead of the bottom 3 in the vertical ones.

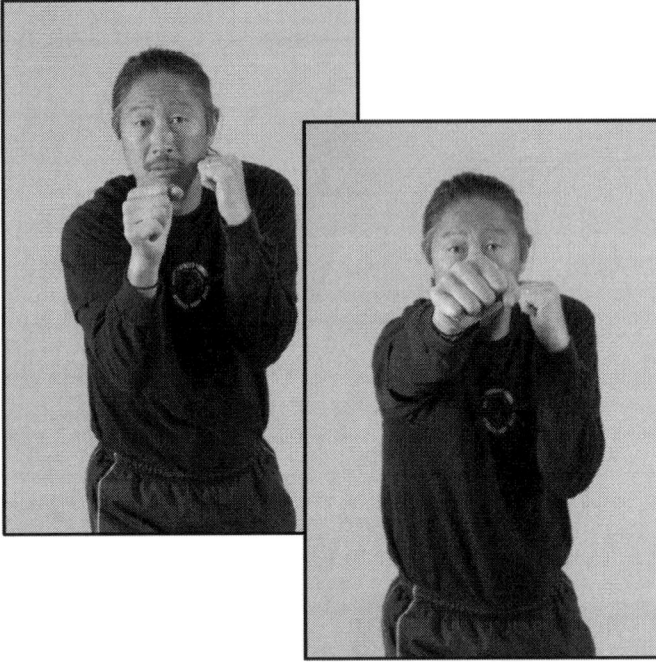

We use the straight lead punch mainly to intercept an attack. Here is an example of an intercepting straight lead against a front hand hook.

If you try and use sliding leverage with a horizontal punch against a left lead punch, you are not able to cut into the tool and your opponent can easily score a hit.

With the vertical fist straight lead you are able to keep your elbow down so as to able to both block and hit at the same time. *LTR*

ADVANTAGES OF THE STRAIGHT LEAD PUNCH:

-- ***It's faster*** – the shortest distance between two points is a straight line

-- ***It's more accurate*** – less chance of missing

-- ***It can foil the opponent's attack*** -- when used as a stop hit.

THE ESSENTIAL QUALITIES OF THE LEAD PUNCH:

   -- Economy of form

   -- Accuracy

   -- Speed

   -- Explosive power

TECHNICAL PRINCIPLES:

To show how much power that you can get with the transfer of your weight from your real leg to your front leg, try doing it with your palm flat on your partner's chest with the elbow straight. Instead of the one-inch punch we call it the no inch punch. The power of this comes from quickly twisting your rear foot and transferring your weight from your rear leg to your front leg. This works best if you have a little more weight on your rear leg.

The *wrong* way to twist hip (shown)

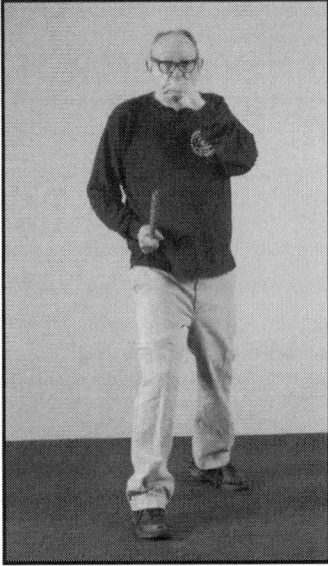

The *right* way to twist

Show foot twist with sticks. With foot twist you would be inside the opponent's punch.

STATIONARY STRAIGHT LEAD PUNCH

For Intercepting --- The straight lead punch is mainly used to intercept an attack with a stop hit. The use of the term "stop hit" means that it should be able to "stop" your opponent dead in his tracks. It requires more distance and time commitment than a power jab. It would not be a good idea to try and attack with a straight lead. *LTR*

For Attacking --- If you need to attack with it, make sure that you are close enough to not have to move forward.

NOTE: The hand does not go first for the stationary straight lead.

Power comes from the *foot twist*, which transfers the weight from the rear leg to the front leg. The rear foot starts the punch.

When in on-guard stance and stationary, there is more weight on the rear leg than the front. It's not 50/50. It's more like 40/60, or even a little more.

Straight lead moving forward --- Show hand first from lead step. Here he drops his hand by not moving his elbow as he strikes.

Entering lead with the push step forward.

FROM NATURAL STANCE:

Replace step. Step forward with the front foot as your step back with the rear leg. Practice this enough so that you have the proper distance for your hit.

Step forward. This time you step forward with the hit if you have the time to react.

Step Back. Sometimes you may need to step back

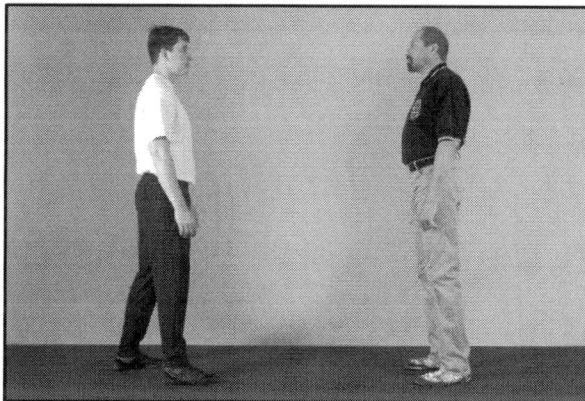

Curve Right if you need to get off of the line of attack.

Step left for the same reason.

Sometimes you may be forced to angle one way or another depending on the environment or more than one opponent.

Drill the above. It is important for the trainer to come in at different distances to make the drill more alive.

DRILLS:

The Basic Intercepting Drill --- In this drill the trainer steps forward with a focus glove. The student can be either in a natural stance or fighting stance.

The trainer should make sure to vary the speed, rhythm, and distance using a push step, or can step through with the rear leg for high punch.

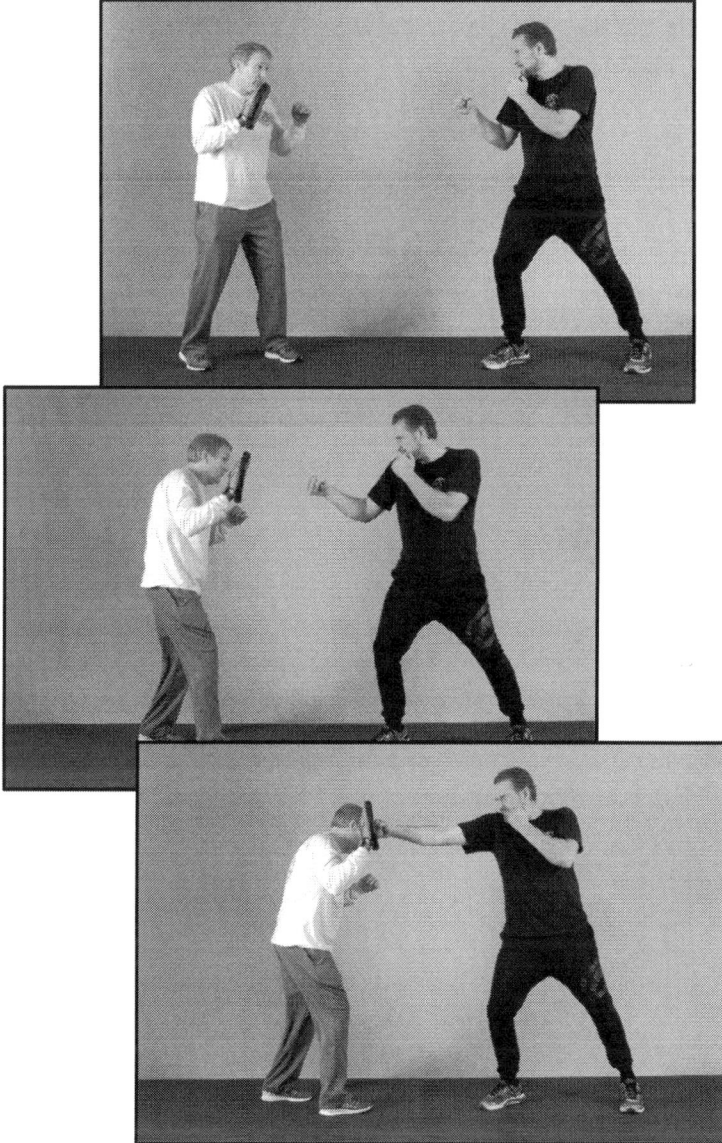

To practice against the tackle, lower your body and the focus glove.

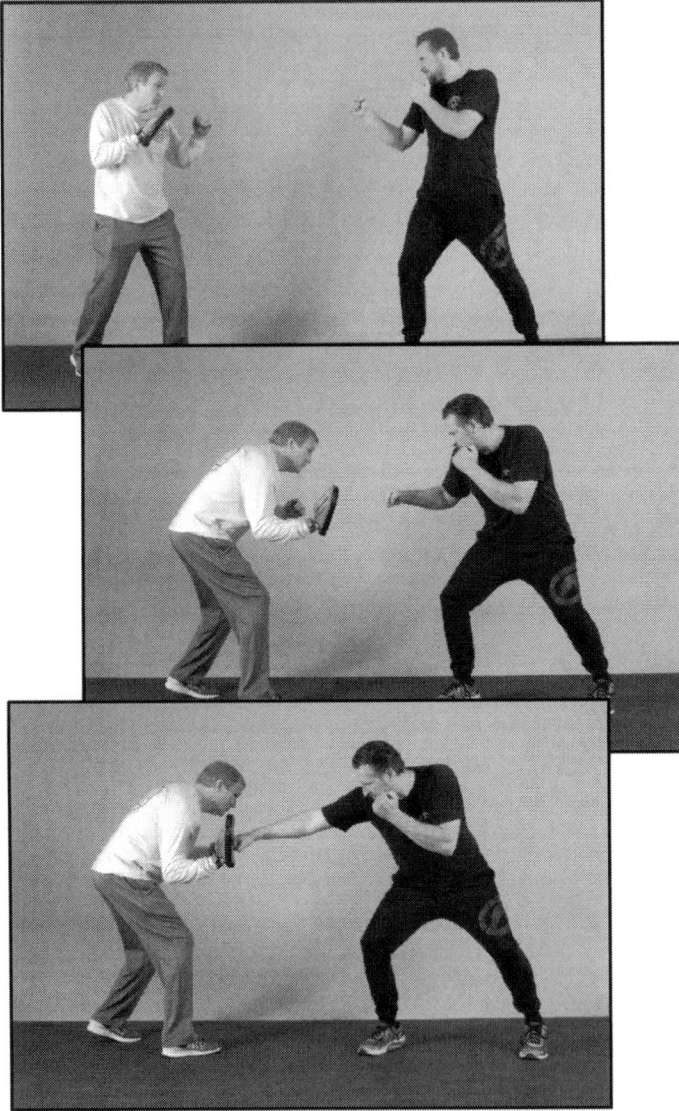

To drill, mix the two.

Dan Lee's Drill – One of Bruce Lee's student showed me this drill. He told me that even in power there must be control. In this drill, you will learn to control the depth and power of your punches.

A minus number 1 punch is used in a combination attack and is used to deceive a parry. To do this punch you must hit as if you were doing a real punch, but the contact barely touches the surface of the target. This "negative" one allows you to do a follow up attack much quicker than a powerful punch as the punch does not go into the target. In the photos below the punch is done with power but strikes the pad as if you were cracking the surface of an egg and not smashing it.

The (-1-2) Minus 1–2 just touching the surface:

No Shoulder Punch: Using just the snap of the elbow, strike the pad with a ¼ inch penetration.

With Shoulder: Adding the shoulder, strike the pad with ½ inch penetration.

With Hip: Adding the hip, strike the pad with a one-inch penetration.

Do each of the above with all footwork and different distances for the punch to travel.

Focus Glove Difference Distance Drills --- 3 distances for focus glove. The trainer sets the focus glove at different distances. The student then strikes with the proper 1- to 2-inch penetration, ending with a snap.

STATIONARY:

LEAD STEP:
With finger jab to show distance – using fist.

STEP BACK PUNCH:

MIX 1 TO 3 ABOVE.

As Defense – Think of focusing on using the straight lead punch as a defensive tool, as it will be less susceptible to a counter.

As Attack, if Necessary – Sometime you need to attack. When you do, you should use the Leg obstruction for safety to avoid his stop hit.

The leg obstruction with a snap to get the maximum power. You should be able to do this hard enough to really damage your opponent's leg.

Angle Straight Lead Punch --- As he starts to punch you angle right and hit.

Angle Straight Lead Punch as an Attack.

Step Back Straight Lead Punch with Rear Foot – stationary.

Step back and slip his jab with a high straight lead.

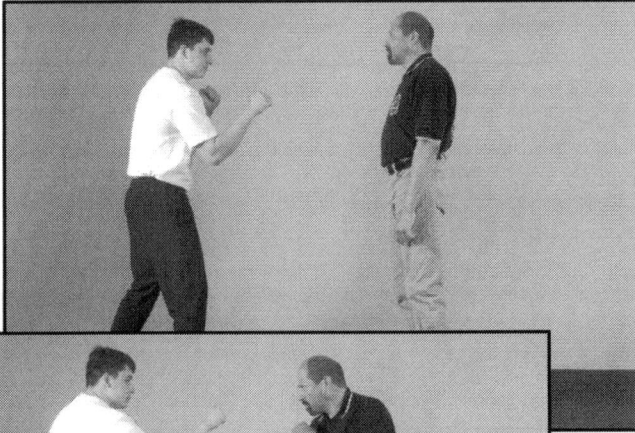

The Rising Straight Lead *-- from Hand on Thigh.*

Straight Lead Elliptical Punch -- using the short arc principle. The power in the short arc principle comes from the whipping of the punch. The punch starts on the outside of the target and then "whips" into the target, which is always the nose of the chin of an opponent.

On an Opponent:

Straight Lead Low Punch -- *with horizontal fist with an outside slip:*

RTR

Outside Slip to High Straight Lead to Face:

Outside Slip Hit High Straight Rear High Punch
--- with horizontal fist:

Rear Low Punch with Outside Slip:
RTL

THE FINGER JAB:

THE FINGER SLICE --- *From Hand on Thigh*:

137

Against Jab -- *Parry and Hit, Cutting into the Tool on the Outside.*

THE STRAIGHT REAR PUNCH:

How to do it:

-- Fist should not be clenched until impact –
   Like slamming a door;

-- After slipping RTR and LTL;

-- Against RTR slip inside.

Hit inside:

Hit over the top:

Against RTL slip outside:

Straight rear low punch with horizontal fist with an outside slip:

RTL

THE BLAST:

The blast is a series of rapid fire punches that or meant to overpower your opponent. It comes from Wing Chun.

While we stress the blast as a way to finish off an opponent. We really stress the way Bruce Lee taught Bob Bremer. While not a rapid fire as the regular Wing Chun blast, it has much more knock out power and gets the fight over with fewer punches.

The Wing Chun blast using basic Wing Chun punches. This is this type of punch is usually used when you are at close range against an opponent.

The Straight Lead – The straight rear blast used when you are at a greater distance. (The JKD blast)

Bruce to Bremer -- *2 shorts followed by JKD blast to get proper distance.*

The Hook --- The hook is usually a close range punch that can be used as a snappy as well as a heavy hit. In a snappy punch the power comes from a fast rotation of the body with a snap back to return to the on-guard position or a follow up blow. The heavy hook is done with the palm and the power come from the weight by digging your toes into the ground.

> *Shown from after straight rear* --- We feel that this is one of the best ways to learn how to rotate your body to get the power need for an effective hook.

How to Drill it: Once you have learned how to rotate your body, you need to learn how to get the proper snap in your hook and be able to shorten the rotation for a more efficient hook. The methods below are a good way to work on it. You may find these difficult to get any power, but if you keep up with it, you will find that you can get knock out power with a short snappy hook.

Elbow on trainer's palm to hook to focus glove:

Arm on Arm Power Drill – Like palm on focus glove, but the punching arm in inside the trainer's rear hand.

150

Close Range Hook Power Drill with head on focus glove:

151

The shovel hook to focus glove --- The shovel hook is called that because it id thrown as if you had a shovel in your hands, and you are throwing what is on it by using your hip and upward angle of your body:

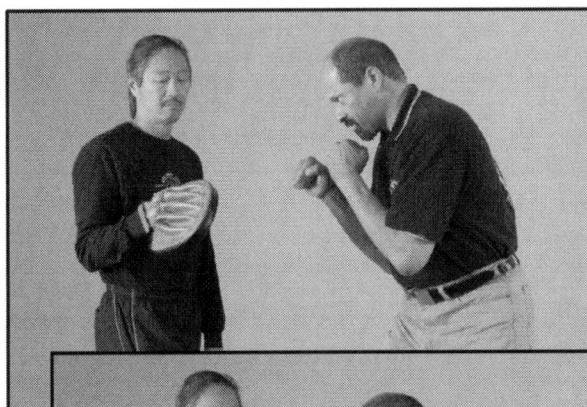

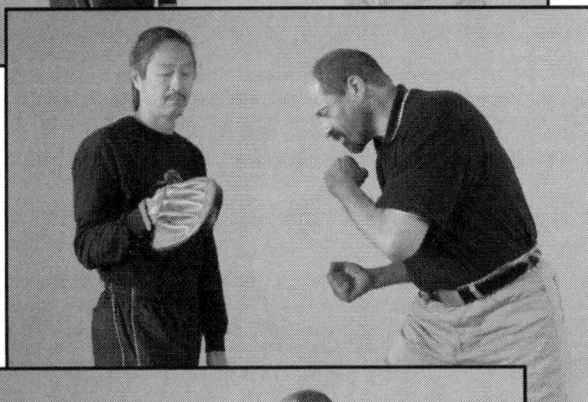

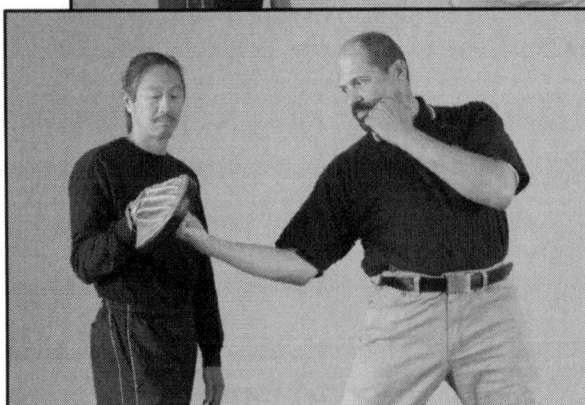

The Shovel to the Body:

The High Uppercut Focus Glove is thrown like the shovel hook, but with a vertical angle:

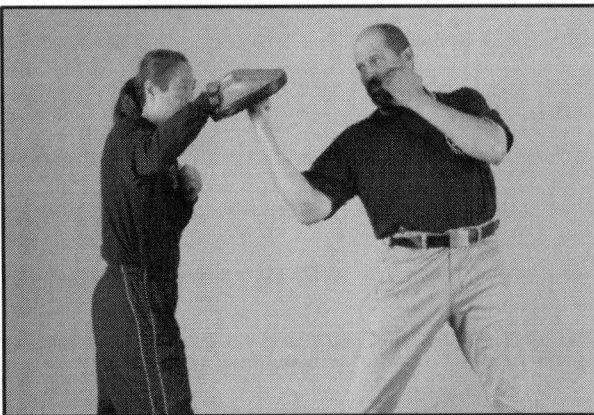

The High Uppercut with Inside Slip to Chin:

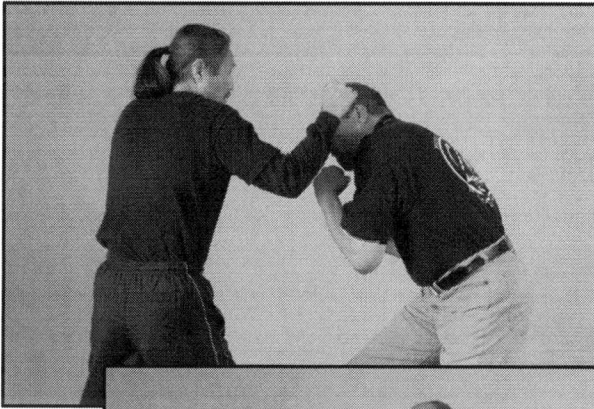

The Vertical Hook

When to use it:
Sometimes when you try to throw an overhead punch, your opponent may be able to easily block it.

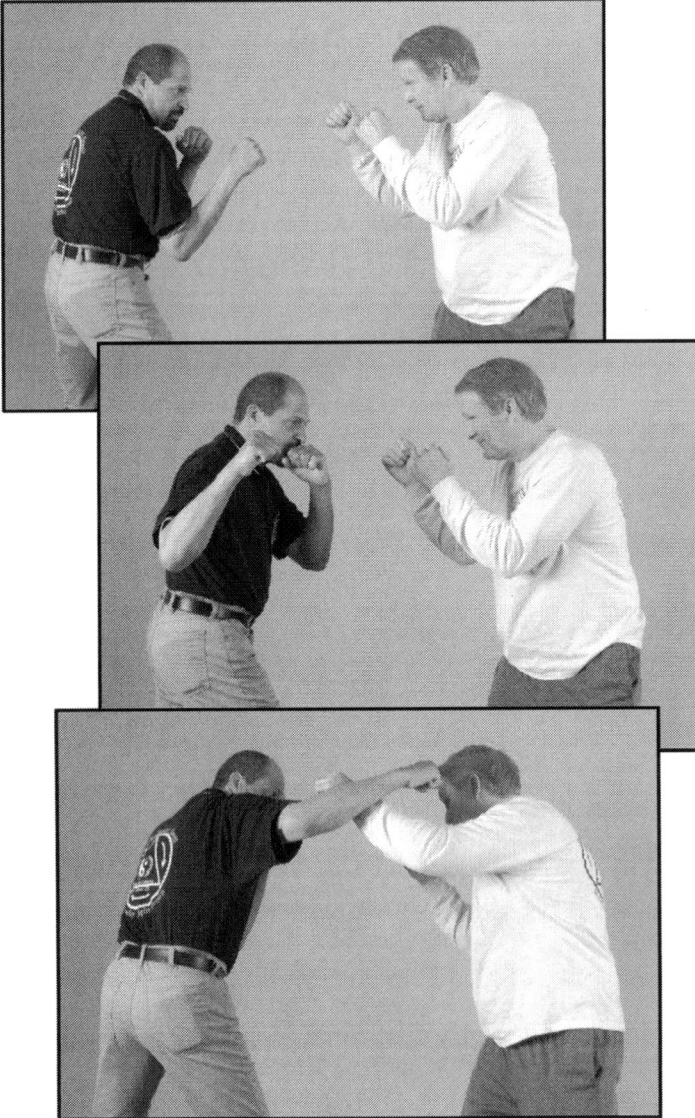

Sometimes it is better to throw a vertical hook with your elbow up so you can hook over the block.

THE CORKSCREW HOOK:

The corkscrew hook is used many as a simultaneous attack and defense against wide hooking type of punch. You do this by using your hook punch inside of his hook. This is not easy and takes a lot of practice.

Against RTL Front Hook:

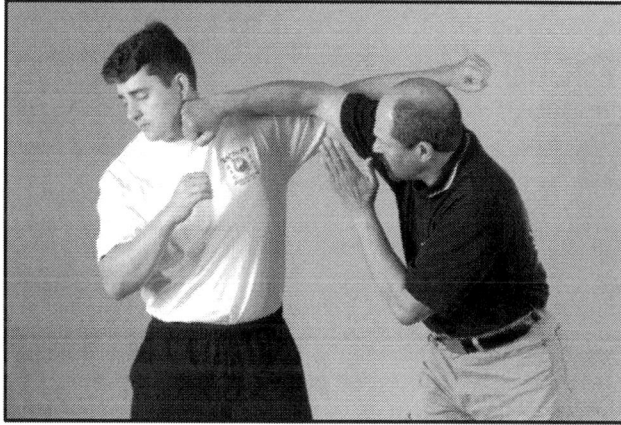

THE CHOPPING HOOK:

The chopping hook is thrown like chopping down with a hatchet. The chopping hook opens the line of attack as you hit.

RTR

THE CHOPPING HOOK TO JAW -- with curve right *RTL*

THE BACK FIST:

Classical – When trying to attack with the classical back fist you need to make two moves. From the on-guard position you need to with have the arm not covering your centerline or move it to back fist line of attack.

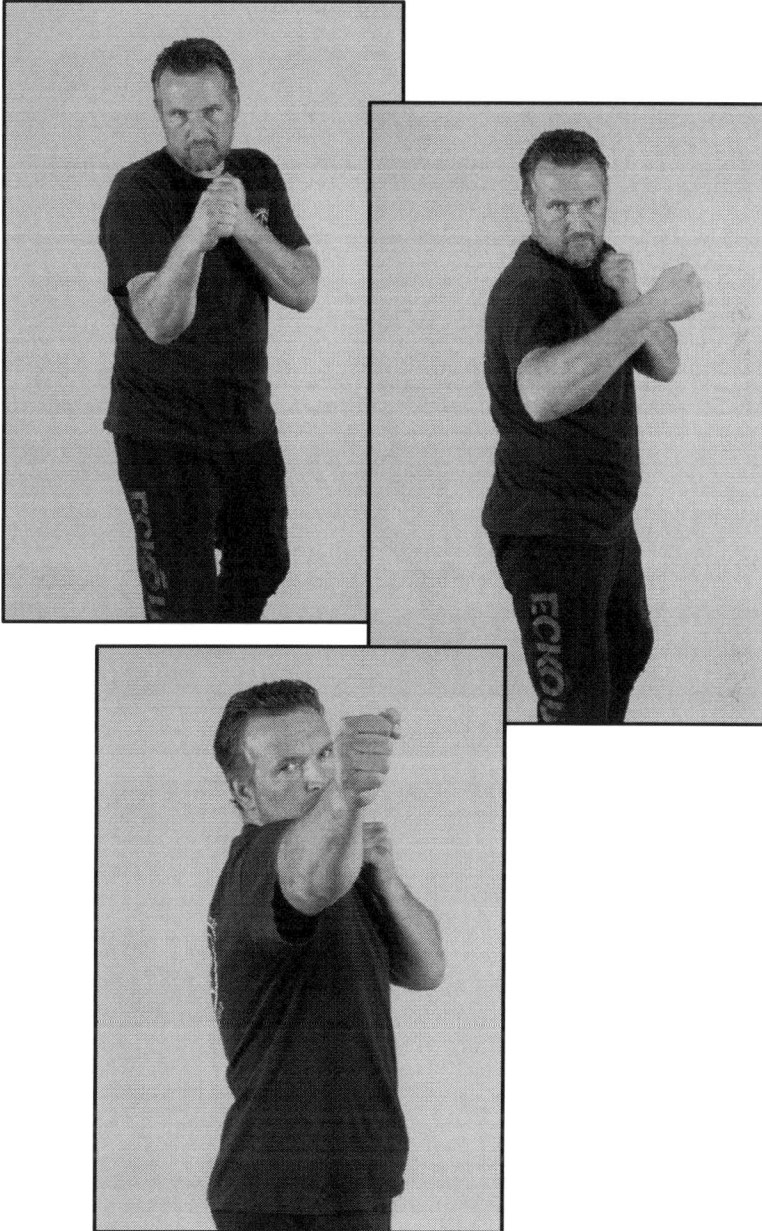

This makes it too easy to counter by intercepting to the now open line:

JKD -- Show fist snap: Instead of hitting with the back of the hand which makes it easy to injure your hand, you hit instead with the knuckles by flicking you wrist as shown.

This hit is not a powerful knockout strike. It is more a blow that stuns the opponent as is meant to hit the nose or the eye. To get the proper angle, you should twist your rear foot as you hit.

Chapter 4

Leg Attacks

BRUCE LEE: *"First use the leg to bridge the gap (distance) then follow up with the hands."*

By using the leg obstruction it is harder for your opponent to intercept. If you just use your hand to attack it is easier for your opponent to intercept as your entire lower body is exposed.

THE LEG OBSTRUCTION:
The is one of the techniques that find essential. It is just as valuable used to attack or to defend against an attack.

> *How to:* Sliding up you kick into the leg of your opponent slamming into him as you square your shoulders and cover with your front hand. The strength of this structure can be seen in a suspension bridge as the square shoulders mimic the support columns of the bridge.

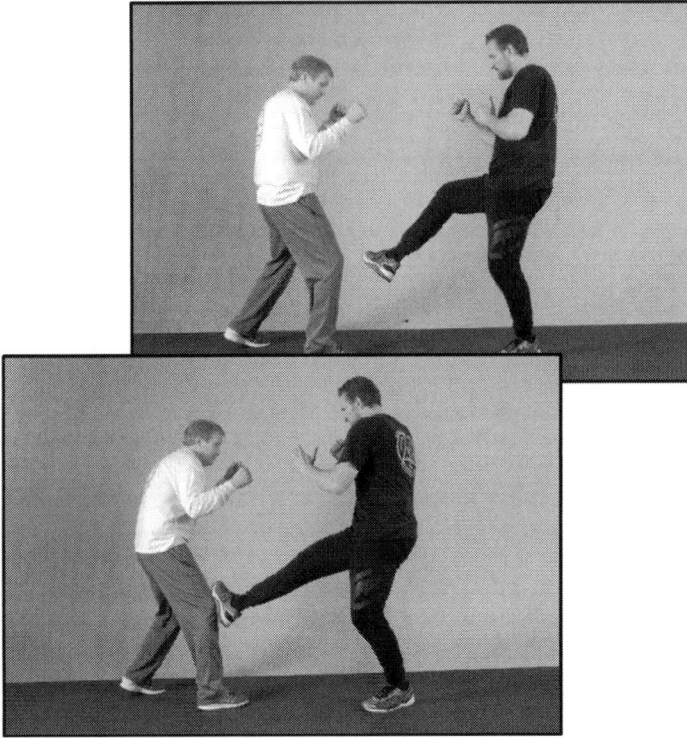

With the shoulders not straight, the structure is weak. Here we can see that Mark can simply push Jeremy off-balance. He would not be able to do this is Jeremy's shoulders were square.

FROM THE FIGHTING MEASURE:

Against Punch – snap rear foot down:

While the main purpose of the leg obstruction is to stop your opponent from moving forward, it can be used as a kick to inflict some damage.

However, if you try to do a leg obstruction to prevent your opponent from advancing, and you try and do it from a side kick structure without having shoulder squared, it will be too weak to stop your opponent from pushing you off balance, as shown in the photo at the top of this page.

Make sure you test this, trying to move forward from both the leg obstruction with the shoulders square as well at an angle.

To Attack– hop up:

To Attack – hop up:

FOLLOW-UPS: Below are just a few examples of possible follow-ups after using the leg obstruction.

STRAIGHT BLAST:

BOXING:

Pop Down with Both Palms to open the line and hit.

RTR - Pak Sao --- slapping his arm down followed by a rear punch. The *pak sao* and *lop sao* are explained in the section of trapping below.

RTR – *Inside Pak and Hit* --- This time, you
trap both of his arms as you come down and hit.

RTL – Cross Parry with Finger Jab:

RTL – Chopping Hook:

RTL – Lop and Hit: As you come down you grab his hand with rear hand and hit.

182

THE SIDE KICK:

Snap -- 4-inch penetration -- You get a snap at the knee for power instead of pushing with the kick.

How to:

Training the side kick:

Focus glove --- Breaking but not smashing the egg.

Shield --- Work the side kick to control your power like the Dan Lee drill on the focus glove as well as the shield from breaking the shell of the egg, to 1-inch penetration, to a maximum of 4 inches. To get the proper snap in your side kick you should not penetrate more than 4 inches. While kicking through the target and sending him flying across the room is impressive, you will do more internal damage by hitting him with a 4 inch snapping kick.

To get the proper snap in our side kicks, Bob Bremer taught us the waterhose principle drill that Bruce Lee showed him. This is done by standing on one leg and thrusting down with your foot and stopping when the leg is straight. You then snap it back as fast as you can as if you were shaking water out of a water hose.

Shield --- One of the ways we learn to get power in our kicks is the ½ kick. By standing on one leg you learn to get power in the snap in just the snap of the kick as the only way you will get any power is by snapping the kick at the knee rather that pushing the kick.

Show at all distances. You need to work on learning to kick at all distances from opponent by the footwork you use to gain the prober distance. In combat you need to be able to judge at a moment's notice the proper distance to be able to kick with the maximum power, so you can hit with a snap.

STEP BACK --- With your hand on the shield, step back and kick.

On opponent:

Stationary --- With your hand on the shield try to kick with a snap:

On opponent:

Short Slide Up on Opponent:

Long Slide Up:

191

Slide Up:

Slide Up on Opponent:

Step and Slide:

Lead Step and Slide --- Disguise the lead step with finger jab as you slide through your front leg and kick.

195

The Burst ---
The Burst is a long range attack and differs from the step and slide kick above in that the rear leg goes through the front leg, which allows you to cover more distance.

The shove to side kick when your opponent is too close. Make sure to step forward as you shove with a snap.

Slide Right – RTR:

Step RT against RTL straight punch – Show on opponent:

200

Step LT with rear foot against RTR jab – Show on opponent.

DEFENDING AGAINST BEING INTERCEPTED:

One of the dangers of attacking with a punch or a kick is that you can be intercepted with either a stop hit or a stop kick. My main teacher, Dan Inosanto, told me that the safest way to enter was with a kick. If you try to attack with any hand attack, there is a good chance that your opponent will counter with a kick to your front leg as your move forward with your attack. The best way to avoid this is to stop his stop kick before he has the time to use it.

One of the first ways we teach to do this is with the side kick. After the kick you can follow up your attack. Below are two examples. While we are showing the side kick to the side, it is best to use the kick on your opponent's knee so the he cannot stop-kick you.

To Finger Jab:

To Blast:

Leg Lift to block any stop kick to finger jab, which is a little faster to follow up with than the regular side kick.

Leg Obstruction to trap and hit.

THE HOOK KICK:

The snappy hook kick is done with the whip principle. You learn to throw the kick as if you were cracking a whip.

½ kick to focus glove starting by standing on one leg. This teaches you how to use your hip and how to get the proper snap in your kick.

Slide to kick glove:

Stationary:

Step Back:

THE JKD GROIN KICK WITH A BEAT --- *Uncrispy*

Trainer straight lead --- Student beat parries to JKD groin kick. To do a heavy groin kick, you do not snap the kick, but instead kick through the target as if you were punting a football.

The hook kick as a simple defense against a jab as the opponent is offering you his groin when he jabs. Make sure to lean back as you kick to get out of his punching range. Then punch:

THE INVERTED HOOK KICK:

It is done the opposite of the hook kick by chambering your kick the opposite way.

RTL inverted hooking groin kick with beat --- Parry the jab at the same time you intercept with the kick:

RTL inverted kick used as an attack --- Slide up and kick with a pendulum returning back to the fighting measure:

RTR Rear Leg Inverted Kick as opponent moves to the right:

The Scoop Kick --- Can be used close or medium range. Flick the scoop kick as if you were shaking mud off of your shoe.

MEDIUM RANGE --- **Stationary Scoop Kick:**

CLOSE RANGE RTL --- *From Trapping as Attack;*
Slide up trapping both of your opponent's arms and
scoop kick:

CLOSE RANGE RTL --- *As defense from Pak Sao;* Any time anyone tries to enter and trap your arms, he will always have his groin open to attack. Be aware of just how many times this will occur in combat or sparring.

The Distracting Ways to Conceal the Kick

SOUND
METHOD:
2 Hand Clap:

1 Hand Extend Other Slap Thigh

Visual: High lead hand out to conceal with lead step and slide.

These are just of few examples of concealing or distracting your attack.

Chapter 5

Defense

AWARENESS is the most important aspect in defense. The hammer principle is one of our basic methods of working on awareness that we focus on. The way the drill works is as follows: The trainer and the student stand apart the trainer in a natural stance and the student in an on-guard stance. How far apart depends on how the successful the student is, as he supposed to touch the trainer on the forehead with a finger jab. If the trainer blocks every one, then the student is too far away. If he hits with every one, he is too close. To make the drill worthwhile, it should not be too easy for either one.

Hammer principle is used to learn how to attack efficiently by first getting rid of your preparation. Most people when they attack have some sort of preparation that will let the defender know when it is coming. Everybody has a "tell." While it is difficult to disguise the step forward to get into range, you can learn to get rid of other preparations. You do this by attacking the trainer. If the trainer can block it, he will tell you what he saw when you initiated your attack. Some of the common preparations are shown below.

To Get Rid of Your Preparation:

WITHDRAWING HAND:

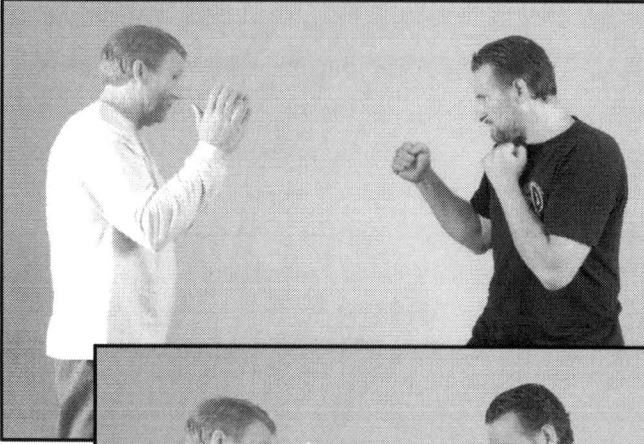

DROPPING YOUR BODY:

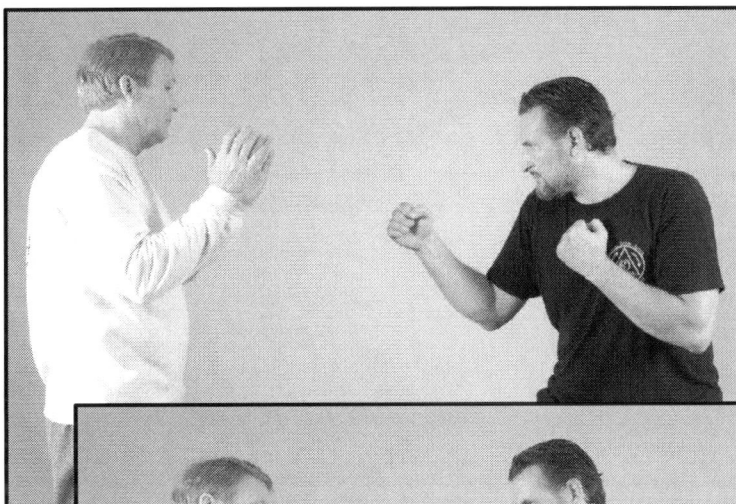

ELBOW OUT:

FACIAL CUE:

Some people may show a tension in their face or change their expression right before they attack.

HAND NOT FIRST:

HAND FIRST:

You need to really work on having your hand start the attack a split second before moving forward. Not only does this help to disguise the attack, but also you will strike a moment before your foot touches the ground. This means that the power will still be going toward the opponent adding to your power.

"*I don't hit – it hits*" is a saying of Bruce Lee's, but not many really understand what he meant by that. Once you have gotten rid of your preparation, you may still find that even though your attack speed is faster and smoother and you are able to do it at a longer distance, the trainer is still able to parry your attack. What is going on is that the trainer is now reading your intention to attack and is sometimes able to hit you even as you are thinking, "I am going to hit now". When you think about attacking, your opponent may be able to "read" this intention. You then need to learn to attack when you sense an opening and then hit without thought so that you don't it. It hits.

The hammer principle can you help get rid of your intention, which includes your mental and physical tension. Your opponent can sense this. You need to have your attack be a surprise to *you*.

Dropping the Hammer

HAMMER PRINCIPLE IN DEFENSE:

The real purpose is awareness. In reality the trainer by making you get rid of your preparation and making your attack better and better is actually training his awareness and will get better as you are getting better,

By working with your partner and getting rid of his preparation, you can really see and attack coming and be able to intercept it. After a while you can "feel "his attack coming. This is the hardest thing to get, but the more you work on it the better you will get. If you try to feel it you will never get it. When you do get it, it will just happen. You will be able to hit without thinking about it or analyzing it. It is a long hard toad to reach that level, but it is worth aspiring for. You may never get "it", but you will get better and better once you work on it. We've found that few will take the time to really spend on this, as it does take a long time to get it.

When Bob Bremer and I would go to the yearly Bruce Lee Educational Seminar and teach there we would work on the straight lead and the hammer principle. We would spend a lot of time on them, but when we would go back the next year, even though the most of same people were there, when we would ask them to show us the straight lead punch, they would have no power in it. We would then work on it again. The next year, it would be the same thing. When we started to work on it, the students would say," Sifu, We know that". I remember Bremer telling a group, "You don't know it. You just recognize it". To "know it", you must be able to "do" it.

DEFENSE AGAINST HAND ATTACKS:

Below are a number to different blocks and parries. While we teach these, as they are sometimes necessary for self-defense, we really focus more on the stop hit or kick. When, for example, you block and hit no matter how fast you are there is a certain amount of time between your block and hit. This time lag may give an opening for your opponent to take advantage of. This really can be a problem if you try and hit against a feint or fake. While the Wing Chun principle of simultaneous block and hit is more efficient, it still is not as efficient as the Western fencing principle of the stop hit. If someone moves forward, you stop kick to

231

his leg. If he fakes and attack you hit him. If he feints you hit him. While this is the most efficient and effective way to defend yourself, it is difficult to do. Sometimes while it feels safer to just go ahead and block or retreat, they are still passive moves. Remember that a passive move while it seems save always requires more tome commitment. It is always better, when possible, to just intercept his attack before he can do a follow-up technique and just knock him out. This is what our training strives to acquire.

A. THE 4 CORNERS DEFENSE:
This is the basic Wing Chun defense.

RTR – *Against a Straight Lead or Jab:*

INSIDE PARRY WITH REAR FOOT TWIST:

OUTSIDE SLIP HIT TO INSIDE LINE:

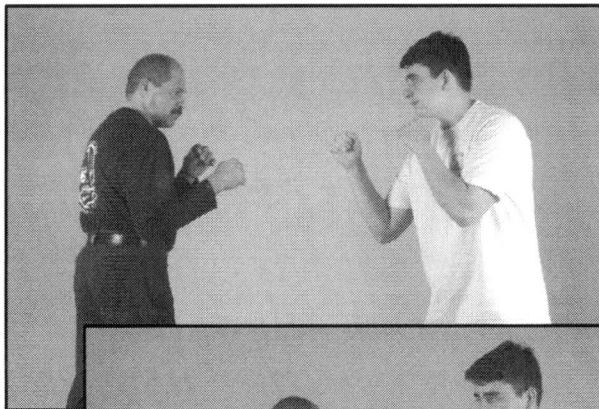

Outside Parry
with Sliding
Leverage Hit
on the
Outside Line:

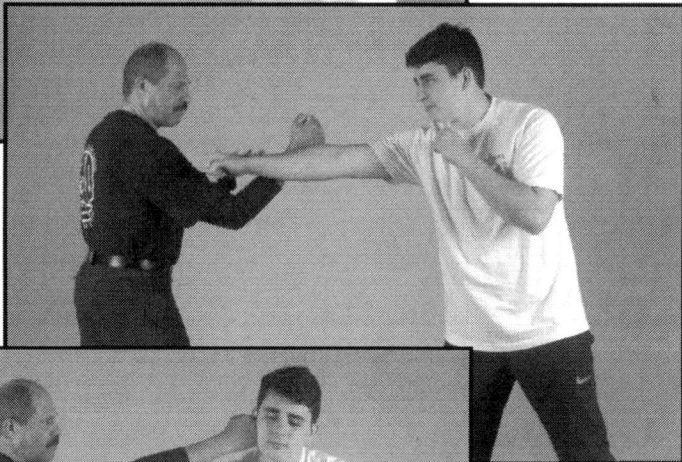

RTR Against Low Straight Punch:

RTL Against Straight Lead --- When you are inside his punch with cross parry and inside sliding leverage with shoulders square:

RTL Against a Straight Punch when you are outside of his attack with outside sliding leverage:

RTL Against Front hook – Corkscrew Punch:

B. BASIC BOXING DEFENSE AGAINST HANDS:

Parries Out – In – Cross

Shoulder Roll Return Straight Rear:

Shoulder Roll to Return Straight Rear and Catch:

241

Catch – Basic Drills:

Catch and Return to Glove:

CATCH AND RETURN TO CHIN:

CATCH WITH TIME HIT:

CATCH AND RETURN REAR HAND:

HEEL AND TOE SWAY --- Drop your weight onto your rear foot as you catch the punch. Then immediately transfer your weight to your front leg as you punch. The return to the on-guard position.

Cuff --- The cuff is done by popping up with your parry, which will open up the low line of your opponent. You can then either go for body shots or a take down.

247

Cover – Boxing and MMA

Boxing – *Show Opening – Ribs:*

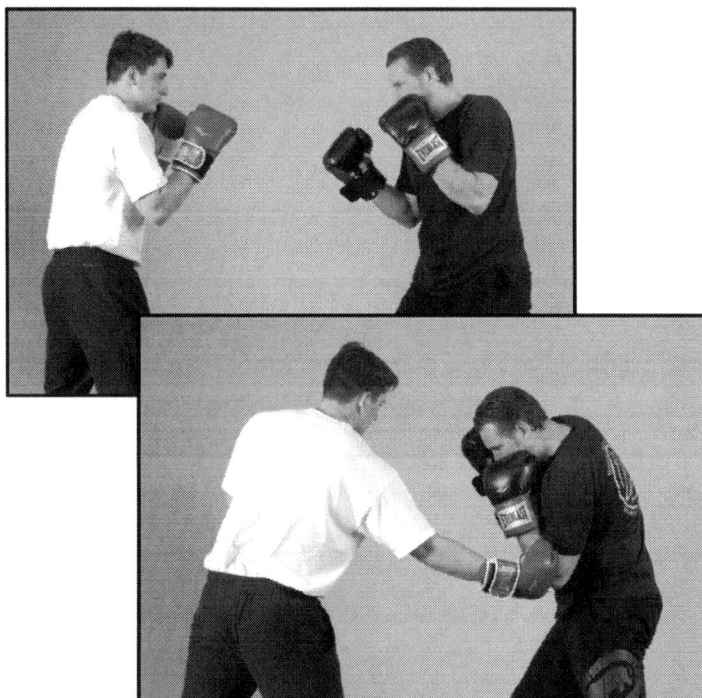

Boxing High Hook Cover:

MMA SHIELD COVER – the problem with it is that all your opponent has to do shove at the elbow to unbalance him:

Slipping In and Out:

INSIDE SLIP AND HIT:

OUTSIDE SLIP AND HIT:

Snap Back --- Snap back just enough to avoid the hit. If you snap back too far your counter attack will be too slow and you are giving time for the attacker to hit again.

Bob and Weave --- Bob LT -- Weave RT

Bob RT -- Weave LT

Step back with rear foot to push forward with rear: as soon as the rear foot touches push forward with a punch. This is an example of broken rhythm footwork as you move forward before the front foot can move back.

Slide front foot back to step forward and hit.

Slide front foot back to rear step up and hit.

Wall Drill --- Bert Poe showed us this drill. It is one of our basic drills for sparring. To do this drill the student stands with his back against the wall. The trainer then throws a series of punches, which the students cover and roll with. This drill teaches the student how to deal with punches after he is injured or pinned up against the ropes. The student is in command of how hard or fast the punches come, by shouting "faster" or "slower" and "harder" and "slower." Once you have done this for a few timed rounds, you can then to working of clinching so the trainer will be no longer able to punch. Start by clinching after the third punch; then after the second and then finally the first.

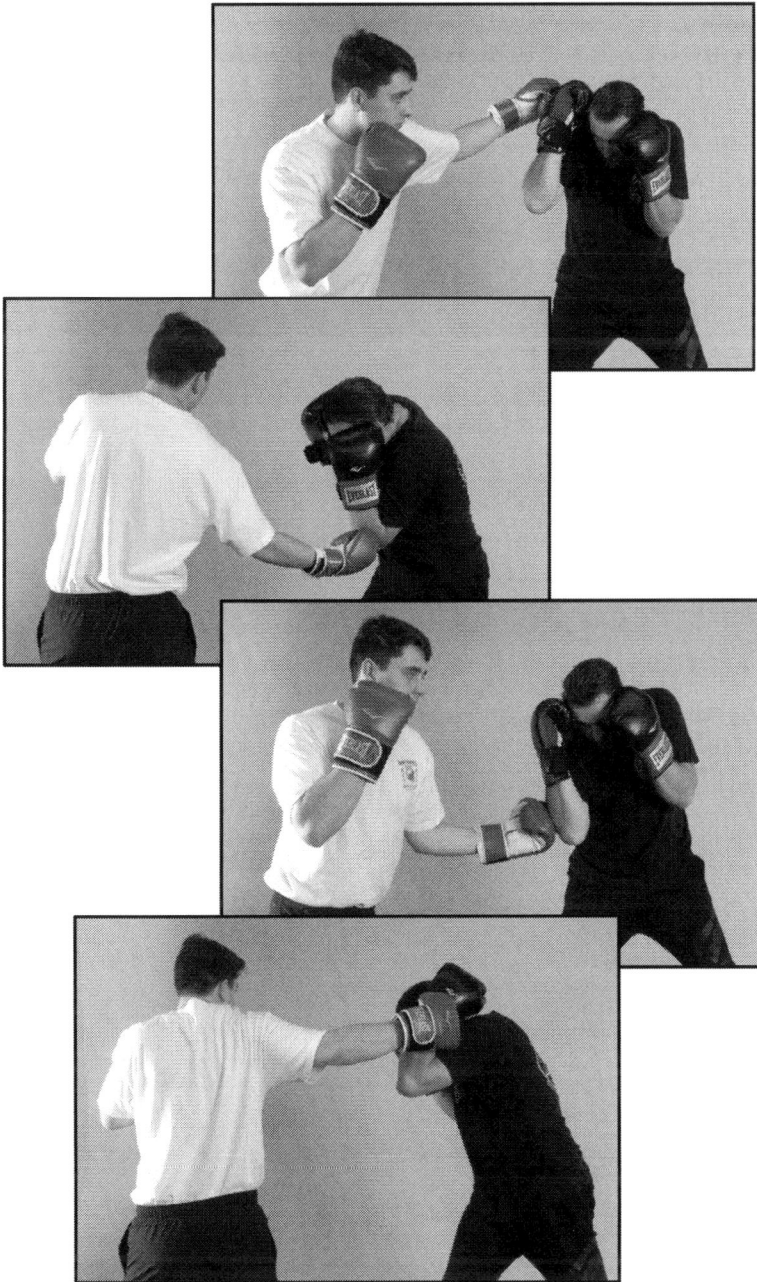

Basic Kicking Defense:

Intercept

Distance

TRAINING DRILLS:

Touch the Shirt Drill --- In the Chinatown school the students would go up and down the floor with one student kicking to the stomach of the other student, who would move back just enough so that the kick barely touched his shirt. The kicker can vary the speed and the depth of the kick. The student then has to relate to the kick and move back just enough to avoid it. The kicker is not trying to kick hard enough to hurt, but the kick should look real. The idea is to learn to move back just enough to avoid the kick, but not so much that you are not be able to counter attack as fast as possible. The only time you should purposely move back too far is if you are trying to draw a second kick so you can intercept it.

Side Kick to Parry Down and Hit:

Trainer Kicks and Defender Slides Back just enough to
return hand before opponent foot touches the ground
(Part 1 of Mixed Move – See below).

Trainer Kick and Steps Down --- Defender pushes back just enough to avoid the kick and returns kick, followed by a hand atack.

Trainer Pendulum Kicks --- Defender slides back
to return kick.

267

Mix Part 1 and Part 2 (above) --- Defender relates. This is one example of how we train the idea of "Punch when you have to punch. Kick when you have to kick." Start slow.

Defense Against Either a Punch or a Kick

The Jam --- While the jam is seldom taught in most JKD schools, we feel that it can be a useful tool to stop an attack in its tracks. To make it work, you need to throw your body into him to smother the attack as if you were trying to smash into him with your hip. Your front leg and rear arm will act as a shield

Chapter 6
The 5 Ways of Attack

SUCCESS OF ATTACK depends on:

1. A fine sense of timing --- Knowing the "when" to hit

2. A perfect judgment of distance --- Getting the proper penetration in the hit or kick to have the maximum

3. A correct application of speed and/or rhythm

4. Attacking with confidence

5. Attacking with accuracy by hitting to the exact spot to be able to stop the attack.

See how many drills you can come up with for each of the above. *Be creative.*

SDA/SAA --- SDA stands for single direct attack, which is one attack that goes on a direct line to the target. SAA stands for single angulated attack, which is a single attack that comes in at an angle to the target.

Technical Principles:

1. BEFORE INITIATION: Before an attack starts, but you are aware that one may occur, make sure you maintain a safe distance from any possible attack, so you can intercept and stop it. Make sure to stay loose but poised and ready for anything;

2. INITIATION: If you have to initiate an attack, make sure that it is economical and done in one continuous movement.

3. Make sure you have THE INTENTION AND THE WILL to hit with exploding force and score a powerful strike

4. During initiation:
   -- Have economical use of movement and force.
   -- Make sure to go for the most direct line of attack. Try to leave as little an opening as possible to avoid a counter-attack by your opponent.

5. After initiation:
   Make sure to have a quick natural flow to recovery or follow up.

SINGLE DIRECT ATTACK OR SDA IN ACTION

SOME EXAMPLES OF TOOLS:

The finger jab with push step --- Any time you are moving forward with a hand attack you should start it by starting by moving your hand first before you step forward. There are 2 main reasons to do so. One is the when you step forward; you are making a large movement that can be easily seen. If you start the hand first it is a small movement and your hand will be on the way to the target before your opponent may see it coming. The other reason if you are throwing a straight lead attack you hit should be able to land slightly before your front foot touches the ground which will add power to your hit from the momentum and weight from your body moving forward.

The Straight Lead with Lead Step – *Hand first*

The Side Kick with Slide:

Below are examples of three different distances for a proper attack. (This is one example of how to train for distance. See how many you can discover in your own training.)

Slide Rear Foot ½ of Distance

Slide Up to Front Foot

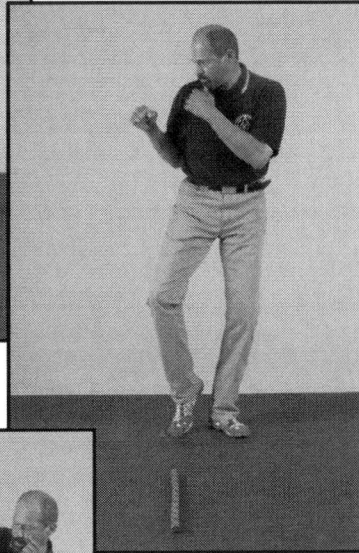

Slide Through Front Foot --- This is an example of the burst.

ABC/ABCWBR:

Some ABC examples; H stands for Hand or elbow. F stands for foot or knee. With this list you can come up with too many combinations to really practice them all. Make a list of all the punches and strikes that you can think of. Then do the same with the kicks, and see how many you can list.

   a. H-H
   b. H-F
   c. F-H
   d. F-F
   e. H-H-H
   f. H-F-H
   g. H-H-F
   h. H-F-F
   i. F-H-F
   j. F-F-H
   k. F-H-H
   l. F-F-F *(Not too common)*

Come up with as many of these combinations that feel good to you. Remember: "H" can be an elbow as well as a hand and "F" can be a knee as well as a kick.

Attack by Combination with Broken Rhythm (ABCWBR):
It is usually used to break up your opponent's defensive rhythm. Notice that when you are sparring and your opponent is attacking with a combination of punches that your defense is in sync with his attack. What you have done is to fall into the attacker's rhythm. This almost always happens if you are drilling and your partner is throwing a jab, to cross to hook and you catch, shoulder roll and cover. Because you drill an attack as well as your defense this way, everything will be in a steady rhythm. Learn to work on breaking up the rhythm of your attack.

BRUCE: *"I'm telling you it's difficult to have a rehearsed routine to fit in with broken rhythm."*

Broken rhythm is designed to help control time in your attack. Let's say that each of these attacks consists of the above jab to cross to hook. Broken rhythm is about controlling your time, which allows you to control the time in your opponent's defense.

> (a.) 1-2-3 = Steady Rhythm as one follows the other with the same time
>
> (b.) 1---2-3 = Jab – Pause – Cross - Hook
>
> (c.) 1-2---3 = Jab – Cross – Pause – Hook.
>
> (d.) Try to do these with as many ABC attacks of three techniques or more

ABC 2-COUNT:

1–2 = Steady Rhythm

1–2 Finger Slice to Finger Jab --- Notice that when you snap the finger slice, it takes a moment of time before you can attack with the rear finger jab. Four photographs are required to demonstrate the move from start to finish.

O.N.E.-2 --- In Bruce Lee's notes on two-technique attacks, he lists "O.N.E."-2 attacks. After working on the 1-2 combination noted above for a while, I discovered that if I relaxed and threw my finger slice slower, but still tried to make contact, that my partner we unable to block the second hit. This is because the time between the 2 attacks has been shortened. As you can see, the attack is now shown in three photos instead of four. If 1-2 means fast-to-fast then O.N.E.-2 means slow to fast. This means that you can break up your partner's rhythm with a two-technique combination attack.

Finger Slice to Straight Rear

-1-2 --- Negative to positive combination attack used for an opponent who parries. When you hit with the jab, try to just barely touch the surface of the focus glove.

1–2 --- Opponent keeps his center line and is able to parry.

-1–2 --- You are able to cheat his parry and score as you can hit with the straight rear punch as soon as your jab is fully extended. The jab is still thrown as fast as possible. You just do not penetrate the target.

+1–2 --- The plus 1 – 2 (sometimes called the rocket punch). It is used for an opponent who catches your jab or straight lead punch. When he catches your jab, the next time you throw one, hit with a heavy hit that sticks to his hand. Then shove very hard to unbalance him and hit with a straight rear punch.

PIA (Progressive Indirect Attack) --- This method of attack is done by throwing a feint or false attack to one line then following it up with a real attack to a different line.

The object of PIA is to:

To provoke a response so that your opponent is forced to parry or use distance to avoid it. This type of attack works best against an opponent to either blocks of uses distance to defend. It should not work against someone who intercepts as when your feint an attack, he should just hit you instead of blocking. Remember that blocking is the least efficient method of defense.

PIA can be used:

-- To overcome a strong defense against SDA
-- To offer variation in one's pattern of attack

Progressive --- to shorten the distance by ½ with the feint
You shorten the other ½ by your attack.

Indirect --- do not wait for the block before completing your attack; keep ahead of it but prolong your feint by enough so that your opponent has time to react.

TECHNICAL TRAINING:

H to Low

RTR HIGH FAKE OR FEINT TO LT –
step up and low upward palm to groin.

RTL STEP LT WITH FEINT -- high back fist to low back fist to groin.

Low to H

RTL FEINT HIGH HAMMER FIST ---
lead to grab his lead and back fist.

High Inside to Outside:

RTR FEINT RT LEAD --- to cut into tool with straight rear.

High Outside to Inside:

RTR high outside strike to sliding inside leverage to eyes.

PIA DRILLS:

Student Hits with a Feint Finger Jab

TRAINER BLOCKS OR PARRIES

Front Hand Block:

You do an inside sliding leverage hit:

Rear Hand Parry:
You do an outside sliding leverage hit

TRAINER MOVES BACK:
Follow with a Kick

PROBLEM – When you do a real finger fan, the hand must snap back before you can hit with your rear hand. This causes you to lose a moment in time.

Try using the O.N.E.–2 as another example of PIA.

Examples of How to Train:

1. Opponent Blocks

2. Opponent Uses Distance

3. Opponent Shoots

4. *Mix the 3* --- *Respond with what happens. React.*
It just happens.

Any time you attack, you will leave some opening for your opponent to take advantage of. You must always be aware of what you are leaving open. In each of the examples above, you are open to a leg obstruction shown below.

Leg Obstruction --- PIA should not work against JKD

RING VS. STREET – Its not just that there are no rules in the street. In the ring you will know who the opponent is and you can do research you can get prior knowledge of how he defends against certain types of attacks. This way you can at least enter the ring with a basic plan of action, but you must keep in mind that you will still have to adapt to what is in front of you. In the street it is all about adapting and fitting in to what is happening in the now. You must be able to fit in with the situation and the environment.

Attack by Drawing (ABD) --- This type of attack is to appear to leave an opening for your opponent to attack so that you can counter-attack. A couple of examples are below.

High Hand to Draw Side Kick:

LOW FRONT HAND TO DRAW HIGH HIT:

Trapping:

The Pak Sao (Slap Hand):

The Pak Sao is used from a reference point to trap the opponent's arm and open a line for your attack. You can do it 3 ways. You can pak and then hit. You can pak and hit at the same time. You can hit and then pak.

The basic pak and hit from reference point done wrong:

Not Trapping the Arm:

Jao Sao Defense --- It you don't trap his arm against his body hard enough, he can circle and hit you with a large disengagement palm hit.

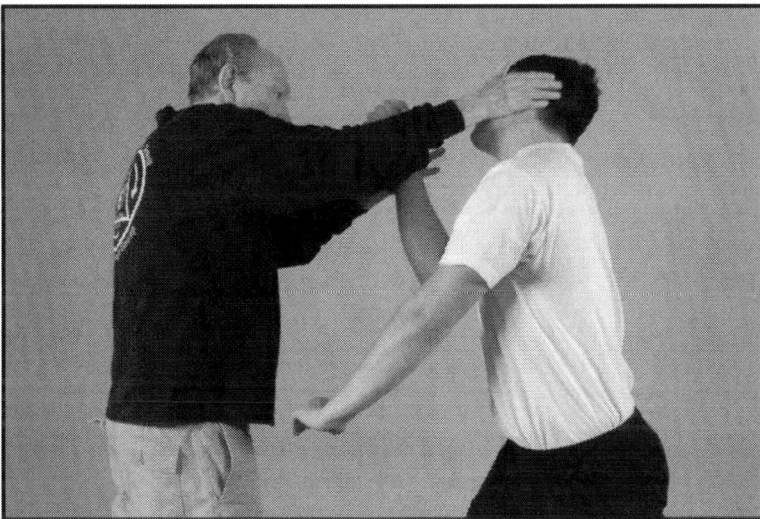

NOT TRAPPING THE LEG --- By not trapping his front leg with your front leg, you can easily be kicked in the groin.

CORRECT PAK SAO --- Both his front arm and leg
are trapped. Notice that with a correct pak sao you
have unbalanced him.

How the reference point attachment is usually taught:

1. Punch is thrown to gain an attachment with his front
   arm, but the hand does not snap back. This is then
   followed by a pak sao. No one with training will punch
   like that.

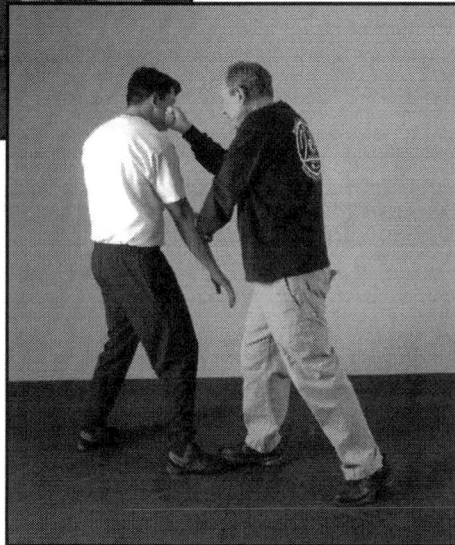

2. If you punch with a proper snap you will not end
up with an attachment.

3. Sometimes you can use a back open hand garbage hand to gain attachment. You throw the hand not to hit but to stick. Followed by trapping the front arm.

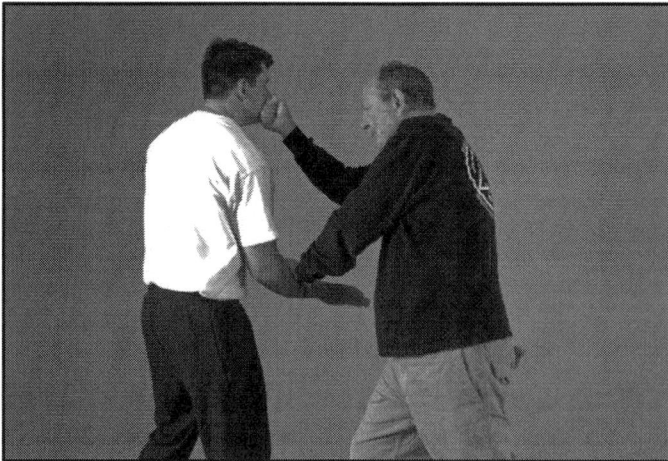

This can be countered easily by any Wing Chun fighter with a lop sao (grab hand) and hit.

The best way to use the pak sao trap is by cutting in to the tool with sliding leverage of his attacking hand. Then pak and hit.

RTR Against Front Lead Punch:

RTL Against Left Lead Punch:

No need to trap as the sliding leverage acts as both a defense and offense. The slide acts as a trap. You can then angle left, trap his rear arm and kick to the groin.

The Lop Sao (the Grab Hand):

Outside lop RTR

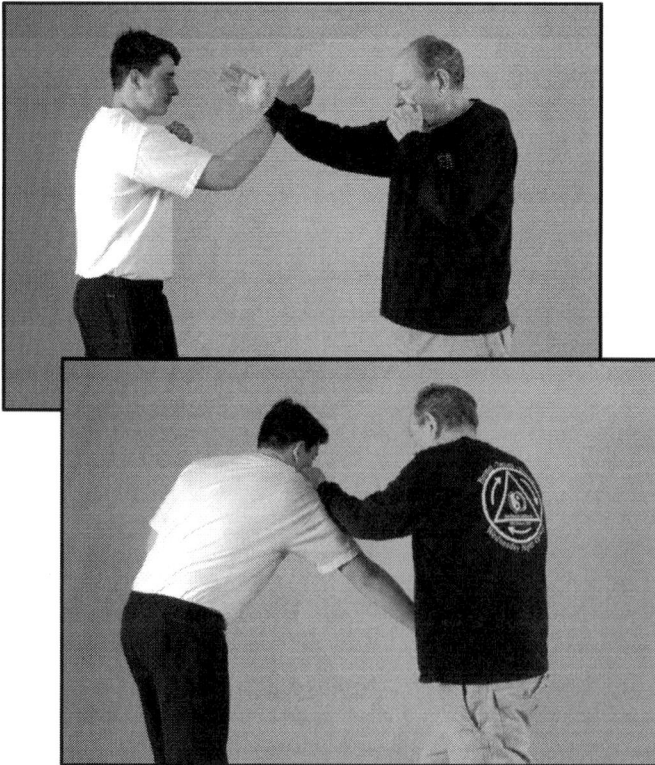

Outside lop RTL

Pak to Lop ---
This is usually taught by trapping his rear arm after your pak with a lop sao to trap both of his arms.

In reality, all you really need to do is blast after the pak.

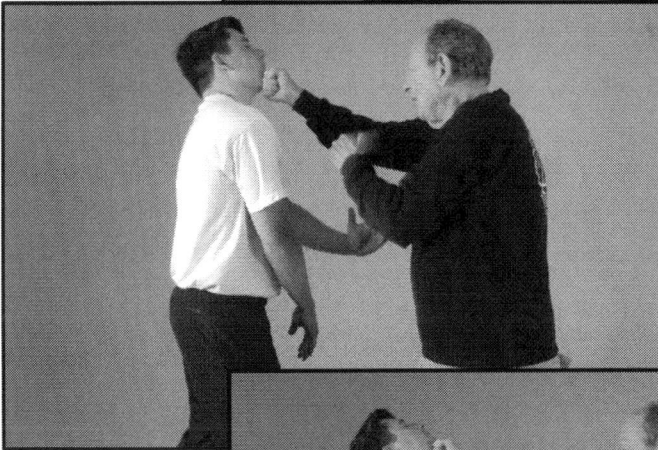

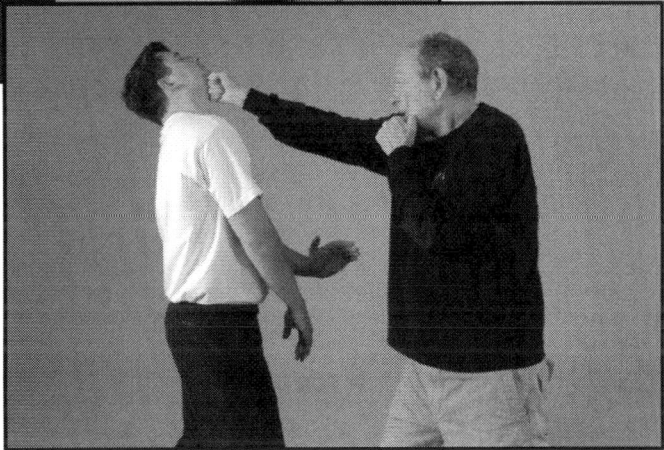

315

When you are in close range, it is easy to lop his arm as he starts to raise them followed by a palm hit to his face.

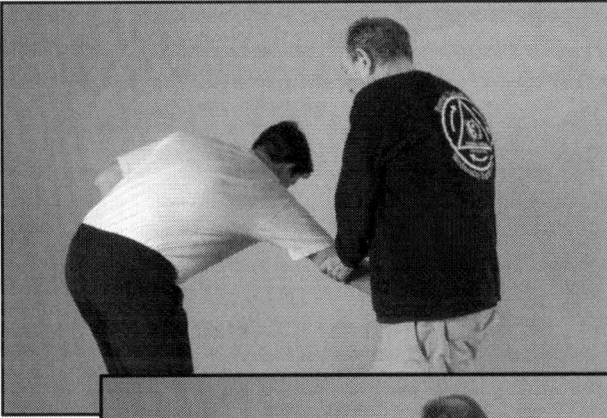

Pulling lop sao to upward chin strike

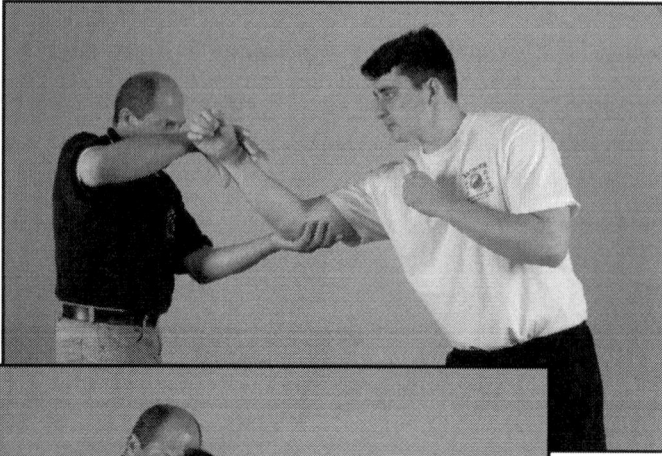

TO DO THIS AGAINST A HAND ATTACK, you need to crash the line making sure that your rear hand is behind his attacking elbow. This is so you can maintain control of his attacking arm as it snaps back. You can then pull his arm down and follow up a kick or an upward palm strike:

Lop when close and opponent has his guard up:

RTR OUTSIDE LOP:

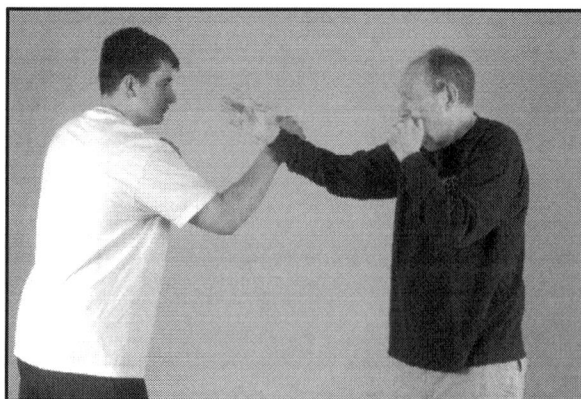

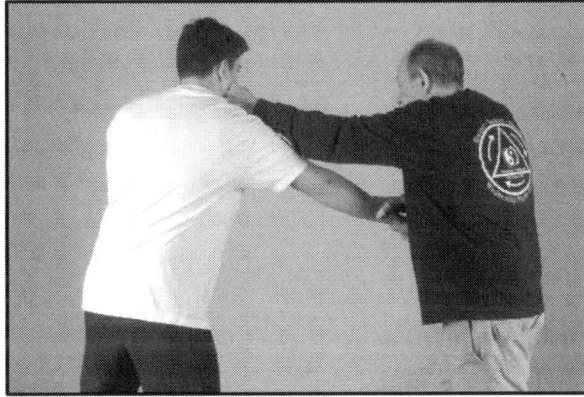

RTL Inside Lop:

RTL INSIDE LOP:

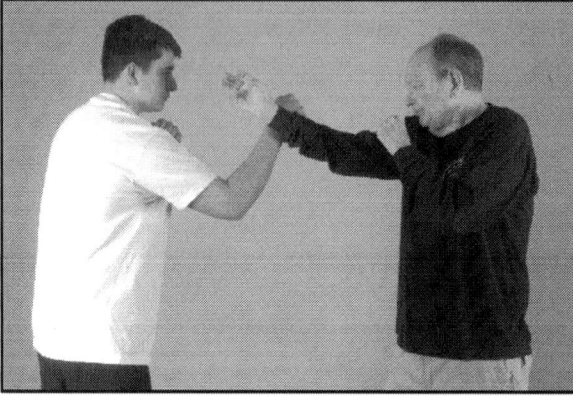

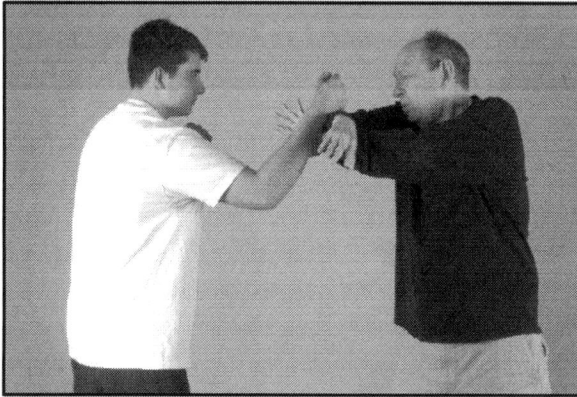

RTR Lop Sao and Hit from Natural Stance:

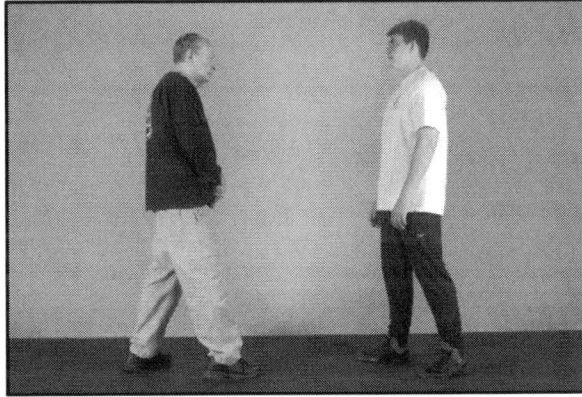

RTL LOP SAO AND HIT FROM NATURAL STANCE:

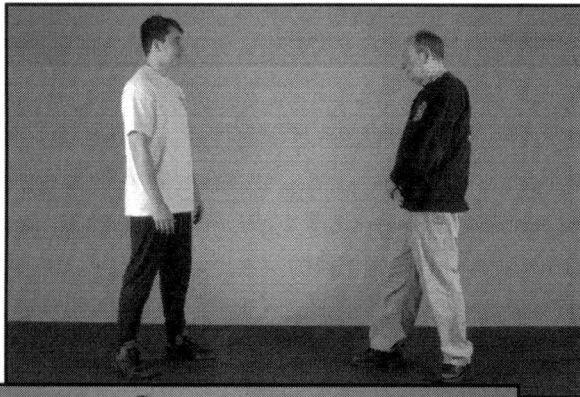

The Lop Sao to Wedge Trap --- Once you have slapped his front hand down…

Wedge his rear arm…

Then pak sao and back hand chop.

RTL AGAINST A LEFT JAB --- Sliding leverage punch, to inside lop sao and hit, to finishing straight lead.

LOP DEFENSE FOR THE LOP SAO --- to wedge trapping attack. This is an example of take what is offered. Let's look at the sequence again.

Notice that when you wedge, you and your opponent both are equal. If he has any experience at all with Wing Chun, he can lop sao your wedge and hit you before you can pak and back fist.

Make sure that when you are learning any know technique, ask yourself, "What am I offering my opponent?" In the example above, you are offering him your rear arm.

THE JAO SAO TO JUT (large disengagement to jerking hand) showing the clicks. Basic technique. The jao sao to large disengagement to jerk his rear arm down and hit with left hand to inside pak and hit. Notice that this take 5 clicks to complete.

330

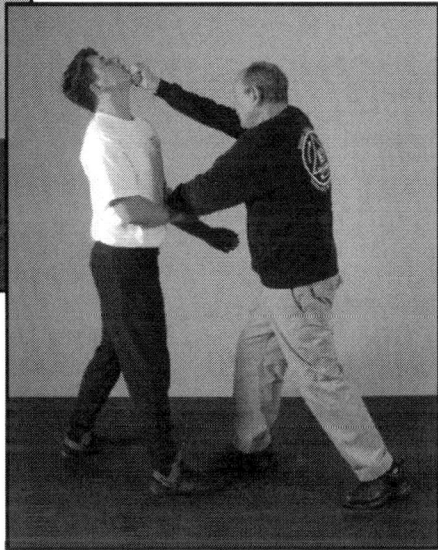

A good Wing Chun man can easily counter the Jao sao to large disengagement palm hit shown in the above sequence of techniques.

-- Reference point

-- Large disengagement to palm hit

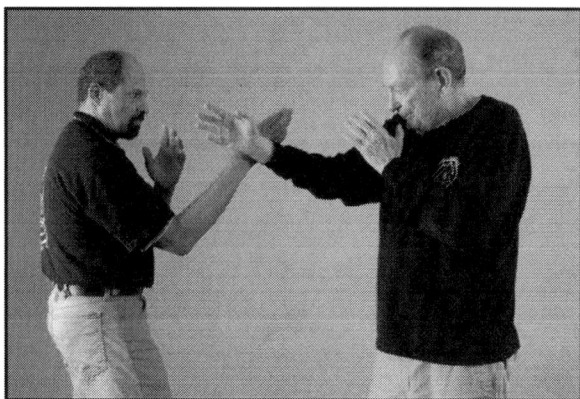

-- To jut and hit.

If you try to hit with your left, a good man with counter with a Wing Chun bong sao.

If you try to jerk his hand down and try to hit him with a straight punch, he will use harmonious spring by sticking to your jut.

You can counter 1 and 2 above by "dividing" his mind by making him feel the jut but instead of hitting with your RT hand you his the your left at the same time you jerk down. *(See basic technique above.)*

You then trap both arms with your punching arm and hit with your RT straight lead.

All this requires at least 5 moves or cliques. With the idea of the time commitment theory in that the more time it takes to do a technique, the more time your opponent has to counter you. The next example of the basic technique removes 1 move or click.

Jao to Hit:

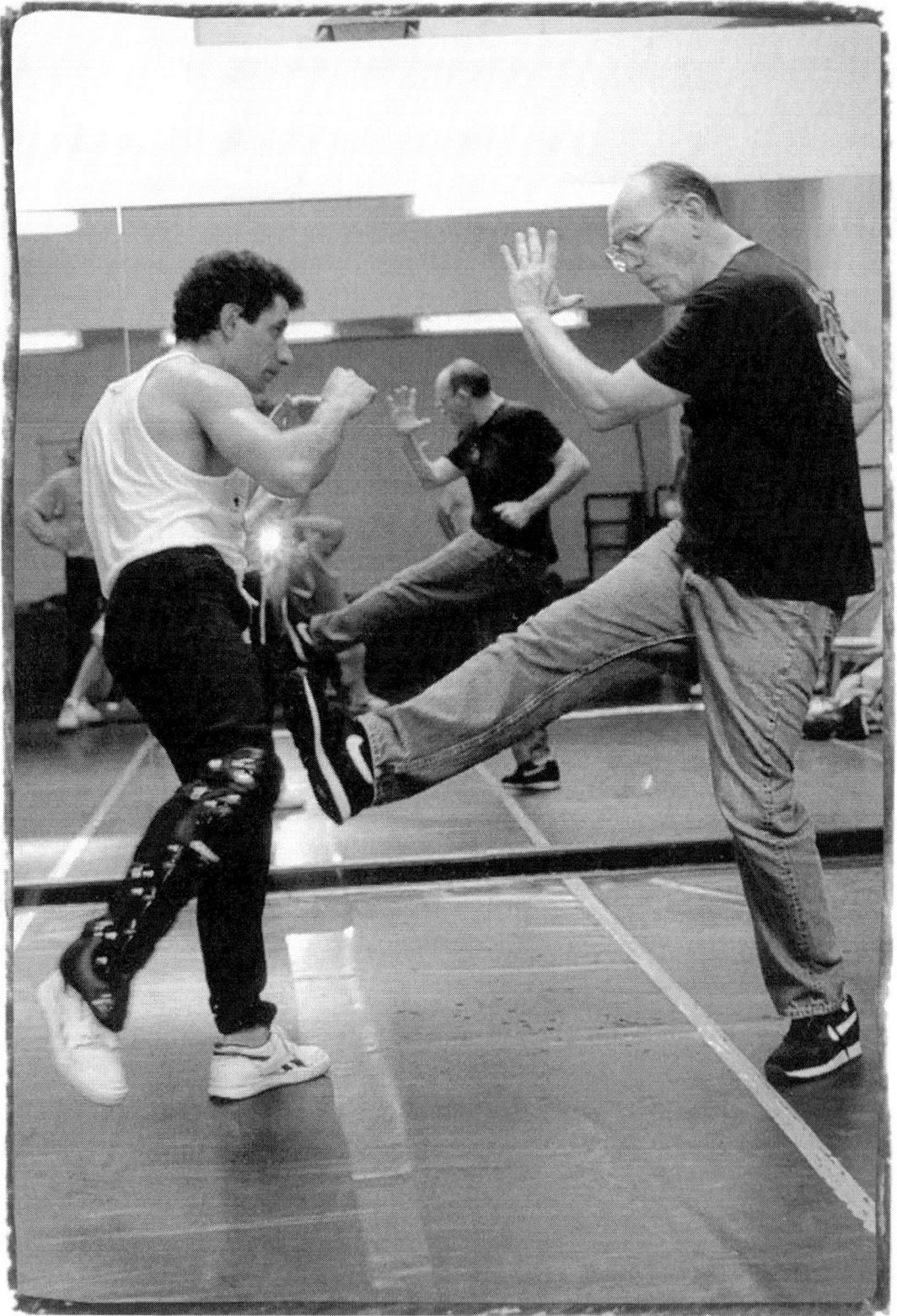

Pull his cover hand down, but as you do this you trap his hand at the same time with your left arm. You are still left with 4 moves or clicks. Let's make it even more efficient.

Jao to Hit --- *The most efficient way to trap.*

This time just quickly jerk his cover hand down and at the same time palm hook to his head. Your opponent will not be able to counter, as it is too fast to pick up. You now have 2 moves as the jut and hit is done at the same time.

These are done in fast motion --- Jut and hit as if you are bouncing off a diving board

Sometimes your opponent will have a lot of mixed martial art training and will use a shield block of the jao palm hit instead of a boxing cover.

If he does this simply take your hitting hand and shove his elbow up which takes his balance away and keep shoving him back as you hit with your rear hand.

338

Some Defense Against Trapping Drills:

BASIC DEFENSES AGAINST THE PAK SAO:

1. Step left with you rear foot to get off
   of his attacking line to your own pak and hit.

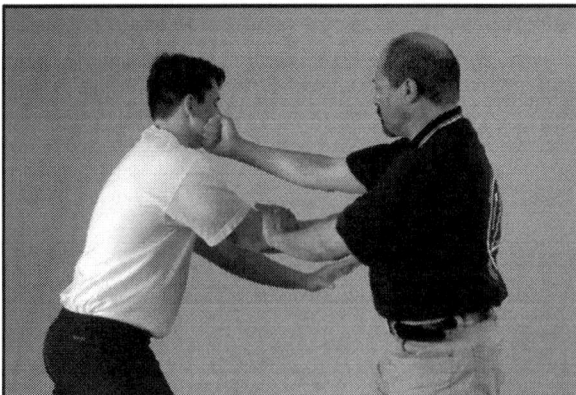

2. Outside sliding leverage

3. Lift and Hit Inside

4. Jao Sao

5. Lop Sao

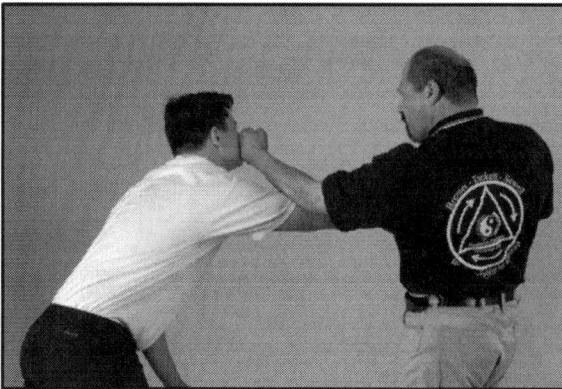

6. Scoop Kick with Parry

Defense against Lop Sao to Rear Punch:

Lop the rear hit to trap both arms and hit:

346

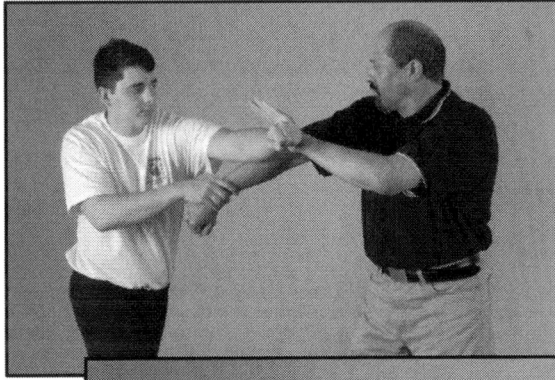

One of the most efficient ways to use the lop sao with a pulling lop sao to upward palm hit as it is really difficult to counter.

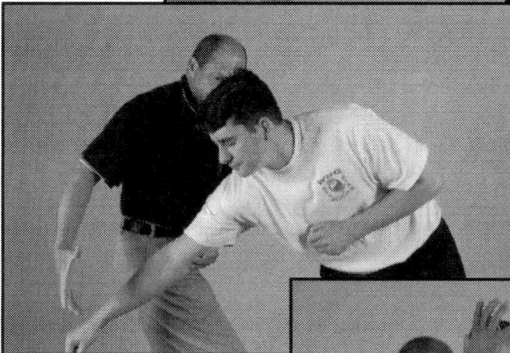

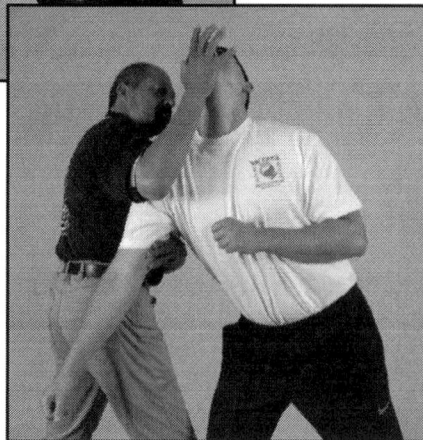

How to Attack Someone Who Intercepts:

When you attempt to attack someone with a punch or kick, you leave yourself vulnerable to a stop hit or kick.

1. THE STOP HIT

2. The Stop Kick:

3. THE LEG OBSTRUCTION --- *against the Stop Hit Entry*:

4. THE LEG OBSTRUCTION ENTRY ---
to Prevent the Stop Hit or Kick:

5. THE SHIELD ENTRY --- This entry should be able to cover enough to prevent most counter strikes. In this sequence, the shield entry is used to jam:

6. You can also use a shield entry to BRIDGE THE GAP AND PUNCH. Slide up as if you were going to attack with a hook kick. Then punch as you drop your leg to the ground:

Technical Principles of JKD to Control Time and Distance:

Work on efficient control of time and distance using footwork and tools of JKD.

TIMING:

Timing in Defense --- (Attack on intention, etc.) Attack on preparation is not an attack into an attack, rather it is launched during the opponent's preparation and before the attack begins.

Control Time --- By using broken rhythm 3- and 2-count (Explained in the section on steady and broken rhythm).

Control Distance --- Work on having an efficient control of distance through footwork practice.

THE DIFFERENT DISTANCES:

When I started working with Sifu Dan Inosanto, we learned that there is a technique that is more efficient at a certain distance. These distances were described as long, medium and close range. We do not use the terms for the various fighting ranges like hand, kicking, trapping and grappling ranges as in reality you can kick at hand range and punch at kicking range. For example a scoop kick can be used at medium as well as close range, and you can do an entering finger slice from a long range if your opponent does not expect it.

ENTERING
FINGER JAB
FROM LONG
RANGE ---
*with a Quick
Lead Step:*

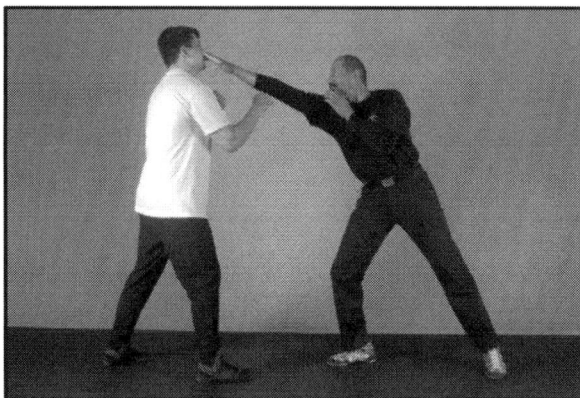

SCOOP KICK FROM MEDIUM RANGE:

SCOOP KICK FROM CLOSE RANGE:

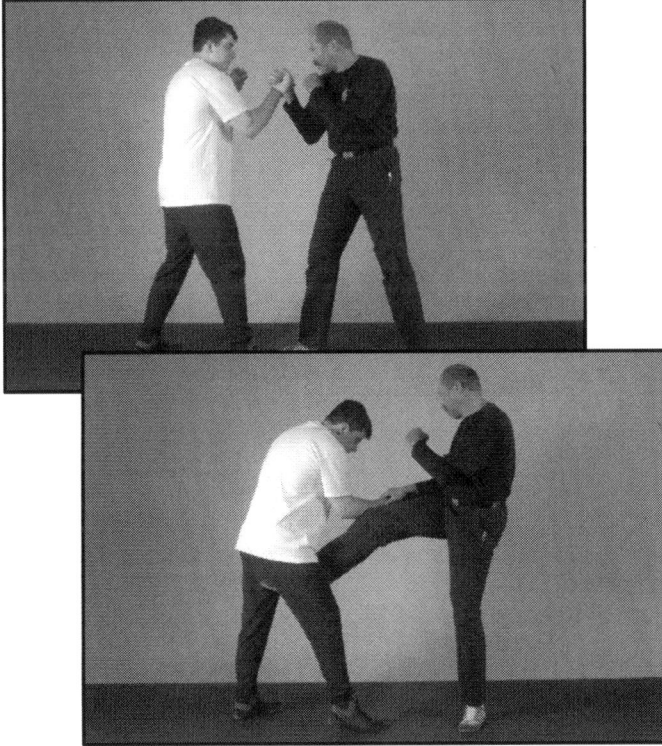

If your opponent has been training that there is such a thing as kicking, hand and trapping range, and has been training to only hit or kick from a certain range, he will not be ready for a hand attack from long range or a kick from close range.

CONTROL DISTANCE

Fighting Measure / Mirror Drill --- Starting from the fighting measure one will move forward, back, left right and circle using various footwork combinations, while the other student tries to keep the fighting measure. When done correctly an observer should have a hard time deciding who is moving first.

EXAMPLES:

Moving Forward:

Moving Back:

Moving to the Left:

Moving to the Right:

Stealing a Step to Grappling Range --- When you slide up you bring your rear foot closer up to your front leg, which gives you a greater distance to thrust forward. Thus you "steal" a step:

Stealing a Step to Finger Jab --- Using a lead step to attack with a finger jab while the other student steps back with his rear foot to retreat:

You can steal a step this time by attacking and sliding your rear foot up, then pushing off that foot to attack:

Try to work so you do the above two moves, one after the other, in one fluid move.

Shadow Closing – This is a drill similar to the mirror, but uses broken rhythm as well as stealing a step and other footwork to bridge the gap and not allow the opponent to escape. It is the opposite of the mirror drill. In the mirror drill, you try to keep the fighting measure. With the shadow closing drill, the aggressor does not let his partner keep the measure and is always working to get past it.

CIRCLE OF COMBAT DRILL --- From fighting measure, have the trainer move around the circle. You pivot. At any time the trainer can attack.

PROPER DISTANCE IN HITTING AND KICKING --- It's easy to learn the mechanics of an attack, but to apply that attack in time with an opponent and at the correct distance takes a lot of practice.

WORK ON YOUR FOOTWORK to be evasive and soft, if opponent is rushing.

PRACTICE FOOTWORK to avoid contact point as if the opponent was armed with a knife. The ultimate aim is to still obtain the brim of fire-line on the opponent's final thrust or kick. Sometimes, practice just using footwork against the thrust of a rubber knife.

> ***Footwork is used to gauge distance.*** And distance is a continually shifting relationship between you and your opponent and depends greatly on speed, agility and control of both.
>
> The JKD man must always keep himself just out of range of the opponent's attack. At the same time, he is constantly on the move to make the opponent misjudge distance and is always ready to intercept the opponent's attack.

Watch for:

-- Preparation

-- Overreaching of opponent

-- When opponent is distracted

-- When opponent is off balance

Vary the length and speed of you own steps. By using footwork you can convert his attack into your attack. Footwork can beat any punch or kick and can add weight and power to a punch or kick

Any attack started from a close enough distance will reach no matter how fast the opponent can parry. The reverse is also true. This is why correct distance using footwork is key.

Footwork = the ability to move the body easily and effectively.

To move just enough will:

-- Make your opponent miss
-- Deliver a counter blow effectively
-- Give you the ability to attack or defend at
   the same time

Learn to move with your tools --- If you can move with your tools from any angle, then you can adapt to whatever is in front of you.

Use your tools to find rhythm and to attack when your opponent is committing.

When too close:

THE STEP BACK PUNCH:
Push back with your foot as you throw a horizontal straight lead punch to his nose. You should strike just as your rear foot lands. For some reason the horizontal feels the best way to punch for me.

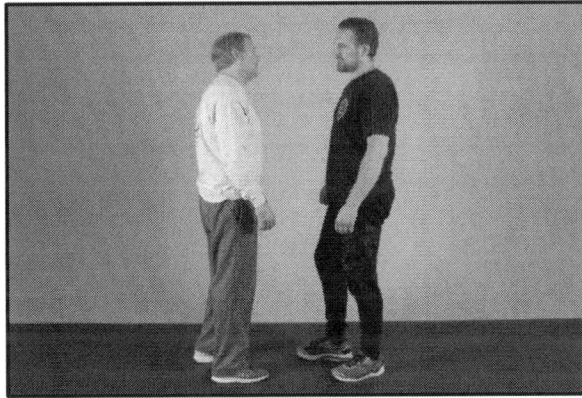

THE WING CHUN PUNCH can be used to gain distance, followed by full power left and right straight punches.

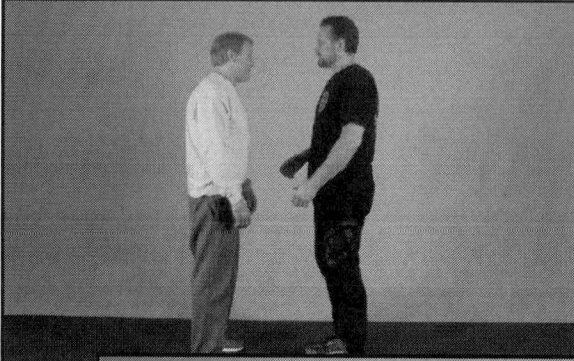

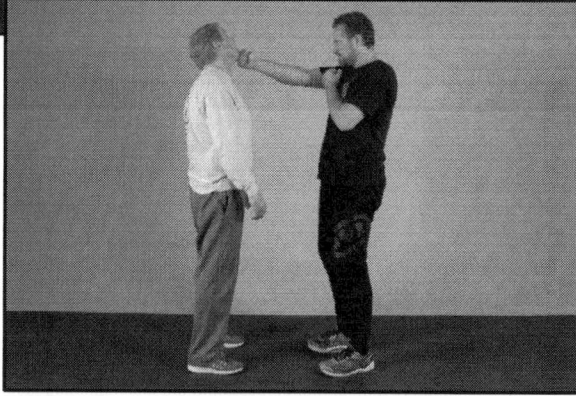

THE SHOVE TO SIDE KICK --- Shove as you step forward with a 2-hand push, followed by a side kick.

With Opponent:

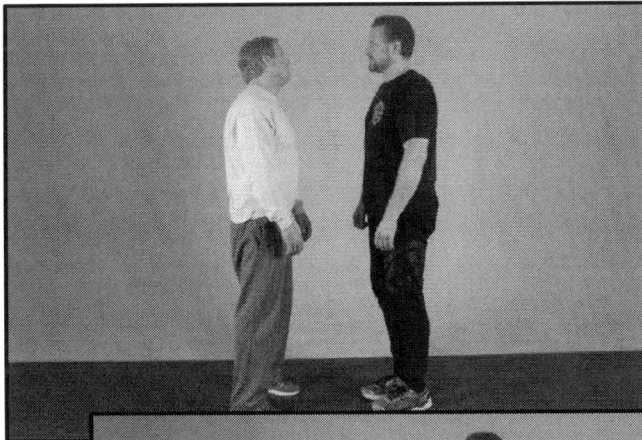

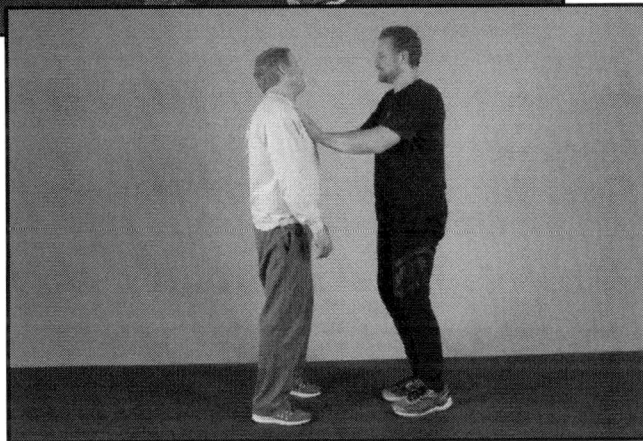

On Kicking Shield:

At a Distance Between Too-close and the Fighting Measure:

-- You can attack with a leg obstruction and a follow up.

-- Trainer with focus glove steps forward.
   Student does a step back punch to focus glove.

ESSENTIAL ENERGY DRILLS:

There are so many ways to practice various energy like *chi sao* from Wing Chun; the problem is that you can spend 80% of your time doing them. Energy drills like chi sao are very important to a Wing Chun man, as the idea is to gain an attachment and control your opponent. With the addition of both the boxing and fencing elements, the focus shifted somewhat from gaining an attachment to avoiding the opponent's contact. Still it is sometimes necessary to stick to your opponent and be able to control him. The question is how much time you should devote to energy drills. The answer, of course, is up to you. When I first started JKD, I spent a lot of time on doing energy drills. Later as I worked more and more on progressive indirect attacks and I found I was working less and less on energy drills. Now we spend more time on intercepting, awareness and power generation and less time on progressive indirect attacks, faking and feinting.

We have focus are energy training on what we consider the four essential energy drills. These are very simple drills and are good to introduce the student to the concept of learning to feel your opponent's energy and be able to respond to it.

1. The High Outside Reference Point Energy Drill:

Trainer shoots hand with a straight punch ---
The student counters with a lop sao and a hit.

The trainer lifts up --- The student counters with parry and low hit.

The trainer punches low --- The student counters with rear hand low parry and front hand strike.

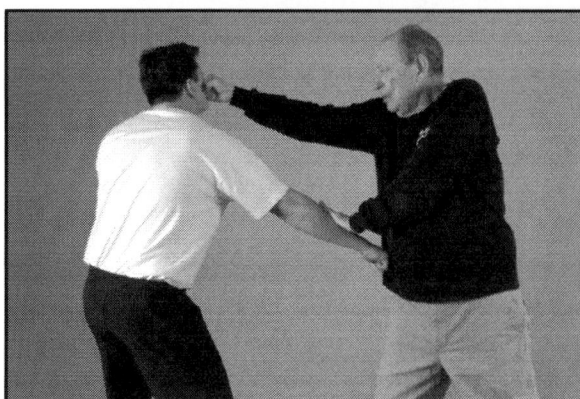

The trainer moves student's arm toward the opponent ---
The student goes with the energy and inside lops and hits.

The trainer does any of the above while student reacts to the energy. Do this with student's eyes closed so he can feel the energy.

The Chi Sao "Take the Hand Away" Drill:

One of the most important principles in Wing Chun is to be able to *thrust forward when the hand is free*. In other words, once you have contact with your opponent's arm and he disengages to hit you, you can counter it by immediately striking with straight hit. The only way to succeed in doing this is to have forward energy so that your hand can hit without you thinking about it. You don't hit. *It* hits.

BASIC CHI SAO ROLL:

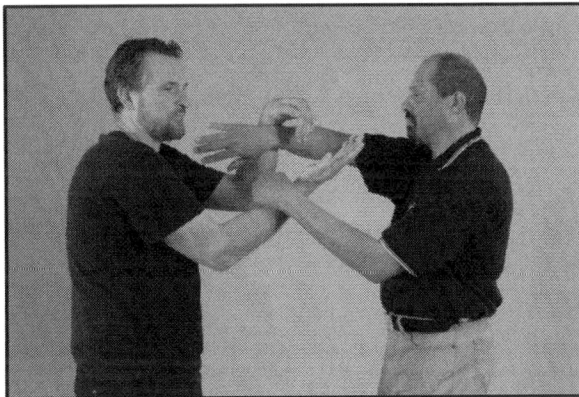

BASIC CHI SAO
ROLL WITH
FORWARD
ENERGY:

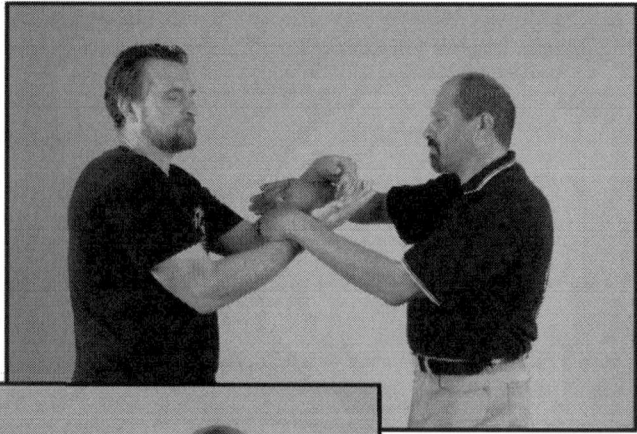

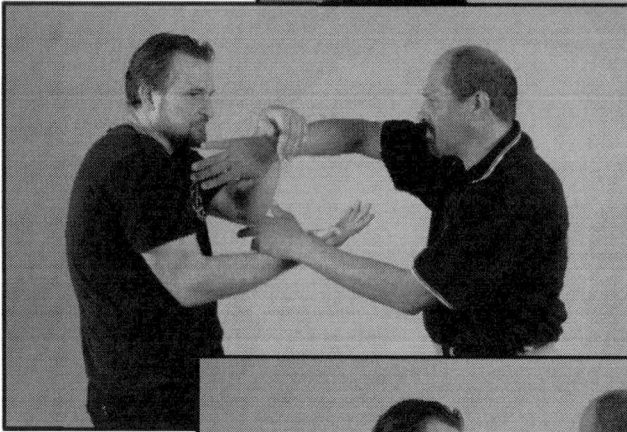

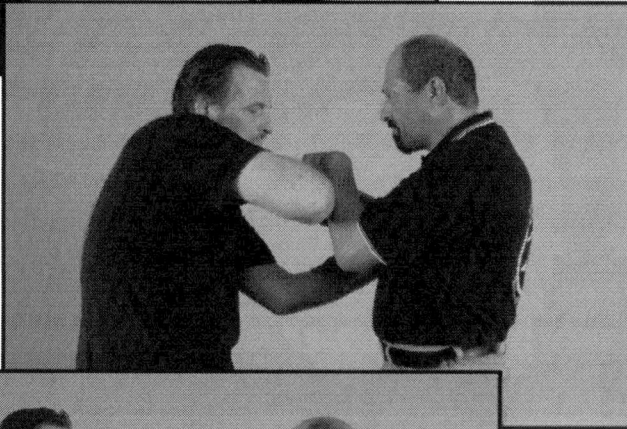

"Take the Hand Away" Drill:

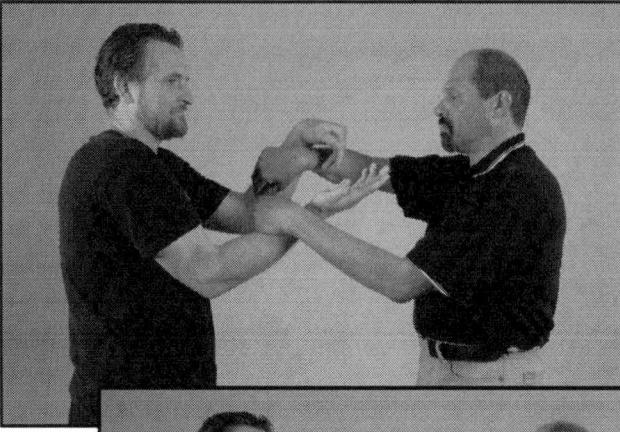

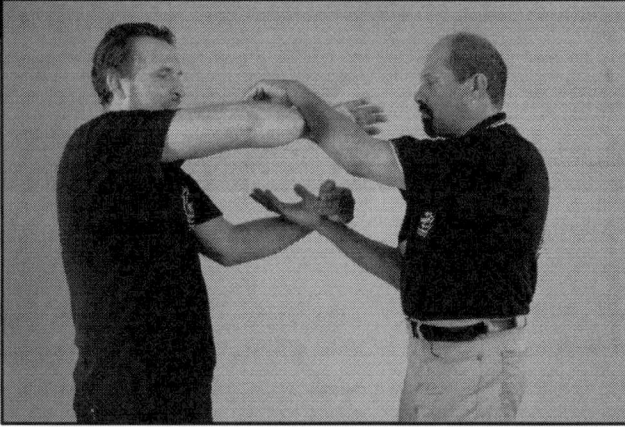

The taking away of the hand is exaggerated in the example. You need to work on it until you can feel the slightest opening. This type of training works with the Wing Chun principle of *thrusting forward when the hand is freed.* First practice with your eyes open, then do the movement with eyes closed to "feel" the opening when it occurs.

The 2-Man Sliding Leverage Energy Drill:

-- Attacks with straight punches

-- Keeps moving forward driving B back with outside leverage straight hits (the sliding leverage blast). This drill works on the Wing Chun principle of *constant forward pressure,* not giving your opponent a chance to count.

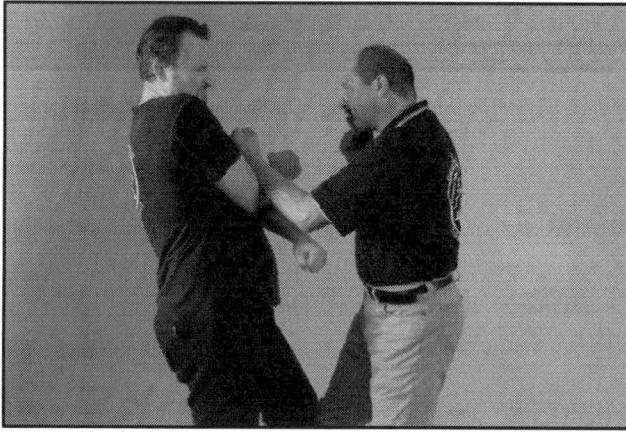

The 2-Man "Grab the Wrist" Drill:

In this drill, the students grab one another's right or left wrists and then try to touch the other's head.

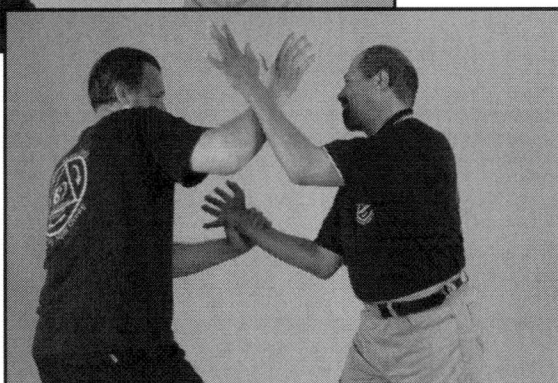

Chapter 7

Training Drills

PRINCIPLES:

(1) Get rid of the clicks.

Try to work on getting rid of unnecessary movements. Work on becoming more efficient.

(2) Get yourself a built in BS detector.

When you are working of a technique constantly ask yourself:

-- What am I leaving open?

-- Is there a better and more efficient way to accomplish the same result?

-- Will this technique work on all types of opponent's or just one, if so which one?

-- How would I defend against it?

-- How would another art defend against it?

-- What are the best follow-ups?

-- Does this technique work on all environments, or just one?

-- Will it work against more than 1 opponent?

(3) 80% of the Time.

This means that you should work 80% of the time on the things you sue the most often. That is your essence of JKD.

(4) Punch when you have to punch. Kick when you have to kick.

TRADITIONAL TRAINING:

The traditional teacher says: "If your opponent does this, then you do this. And then you do this…"

And when you are remembering all the '*and then*'s the other guy is killing you.

SPARRING:

Start slow. Then add intensity and power gradually.

DRILLS:

A. Trainer uses front hand only. Student just defends.

B. Both only use front hand only.

C. 1 all feet – 2 all hands.

D. Both use just front hand and leg.

E. 1 uses both hands – 2 just defends.

F. 1 uses front hand only – 2 rear hand only.

G. In the dark.

(5) Different environment:

    -- Size of room

    -- Furniture

    -- Outdoors

    -- Create as many as you think best.

(6) Discover your own

(7) Multiple opponents sparring

BRUCE LEE notes on fighting more than one man:

"Quickly finish leader first --- Attack to the side and use man as a shield --- When close, use hands in combinations --- When kicking, distance use combinations of kicking."

DRILLS:

-- *2 men on one man*

-- *4 on 2*

-- *3 on 2*

-- *4 men on only exit to an alley; 2 men must fight their way out*

-- *Create your own*

The best way to learn to swim is to get in the water and swim. The best way to learn JKD is to spar. Only in free sparring can a student learn broken rhythm and the exact timing and correct judgment of distance.

When Teaching, Focus on:

1. How it is done;

2. Why it is done; and,

3. When it is done.

THE TEACHING PROGRESSION:

Footwork --- what footwork works with what tool?

Tool Development --- what exercises and drills can I come up with how to get more speed, power and efficiency?

What is the best way to attack with this?

What is the best way to defend against this?

How can I counterattack with it?

Tactics and Strategy:

A. *What type of opponent is this the best against?*

B. *What type of opponent is the most dangerous against this?*

C. *Would the environment affect the technique?*

D. *Is this the best tool for this situation?*

E. *What others can you come up with?*

F. *Understand distance and rhythm in training:*

When the student is working on a drill, they will have a tendency to do it at the same distance and at a steady rhythm. To keep the drill more alive, make sure that the students keep changing the distance and rhythm when work on attack and defense and the feeding of equipment training.

G. *When training a drill in a class situation,* there is a tendency to focus so much on what you are working on that you lose track as to what is going on in your environment. This is a bad idea because in a street situation it is dangerous to focus so much on the potential opponent that you lose track of what else is going on around you in your peripheral vision.

Tai Chi and Hsing-I --- I came to JKD with these as part of my self-defense skills and art. Some of the techniques from these arts fit in with the JKD structure and have added some valuable tools to my essence of JKD.

POINTS TO ADDING TO YOUR JKD:

Why add?

-- You discover that you do not have a good answer for a particular attack.

-- You need to work on defending against grappling.
   a. *How to get back on your feet if taken to the ground.*
   b. *How to avoid the takedown.*

-- It fills a hole that you might have against a certain type of attack.

-- It adds a useful tool. For me, *hsing-i* helped give me the way to use heavy hitting.

JKD FILTER *(see below)* --- Use the basic principles of JKD to analyze any technique or tool you might be thinking of. Does what you add fit in with your JKD structure or not?

HEAVY HITTING --- Heavy hitting is hitting with an "uncrispy" and very heavy hit. A heavy hit commits more time than a snappy-crispy one. This means that while it is a heavy finishing type of hit, which means that you need to be sure you are going to hit the target, your recovery time is slower than a snappy punch. It is a useful blow to use as a follow up to a snappy blow that dazes the opponent.

Hsing-i --- I leaned this from of heavy hitting in Taiwan from two hsing-i teachers. I've kept these techniques as I have found them useful and they fit in with our JKD.

Horizontal Palm ---
Relaxed arm. Think of it as very heavy when you swing and make sure that you dig so that the power comes from the floor your toes into the ground.

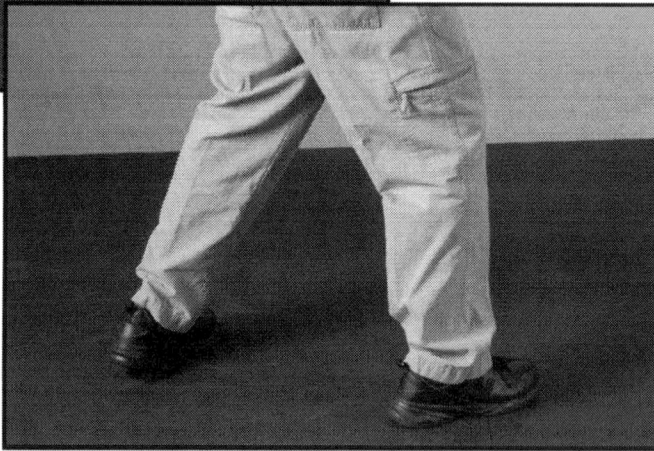

Palm Smash --- with a heavy palm you smash down by dropping your weight as you drop your palm.

Willow Leaf Palm --- this hit is done by shooting a finger jab not meant to hit the eyes. Rather you aim for your opponent's eyebrows catching his nose with the meat near the bottom of your palm. This will smash his nose as you hit through the target.

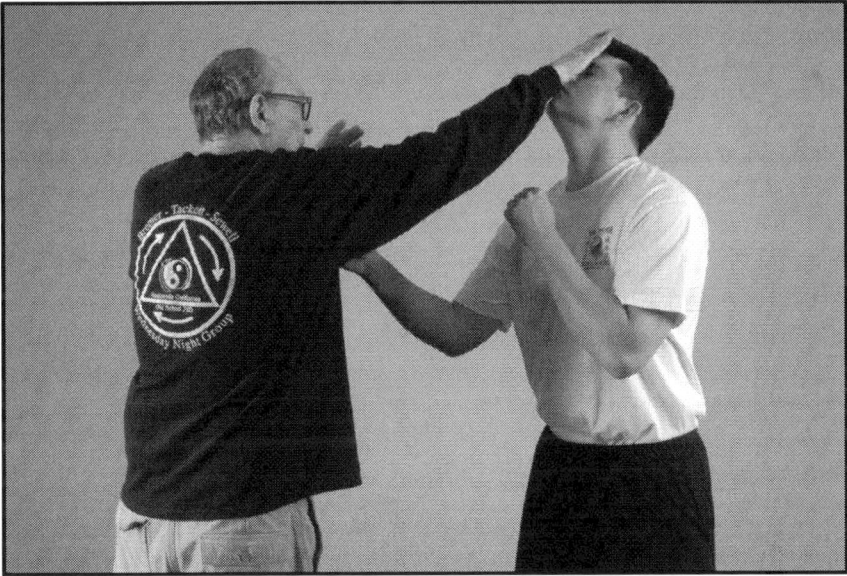

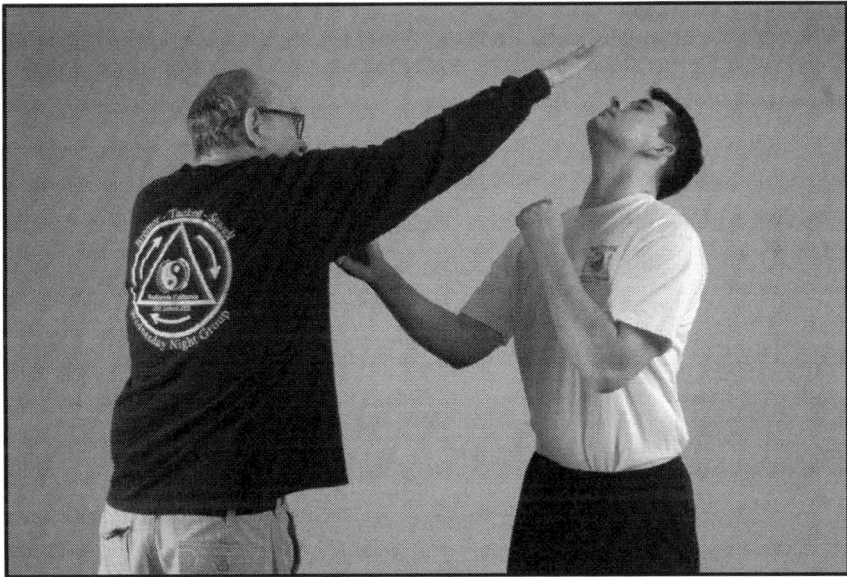

CLOSEUP OF HIT:

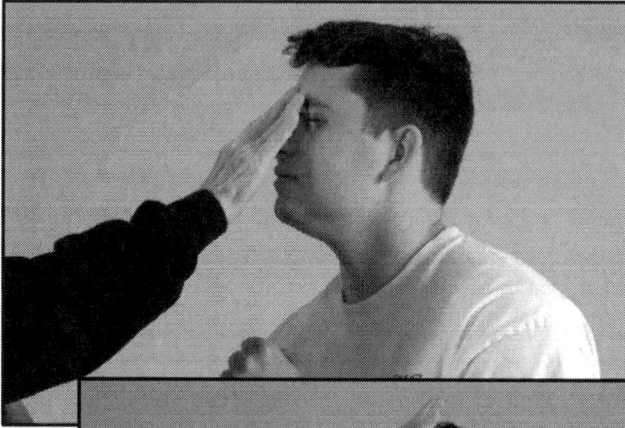

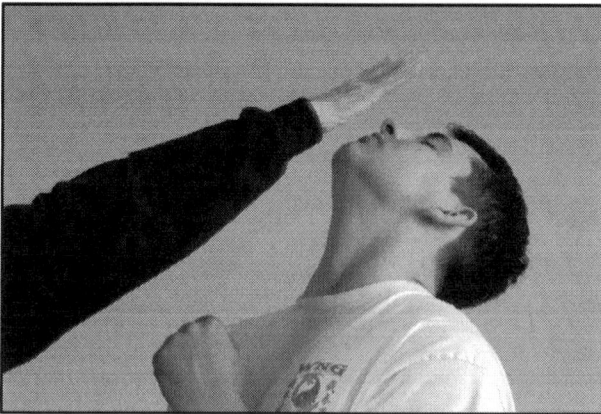

Palm Hook --- this is thrown like boxing hook except that you hit thru the target digging your toes into the ground instead of rotating your body.

Hsing-I Trapping:

DOWNWARD PALM:

Press his front arm down to upward palm smash to the chin to push his head back, followed with a rear downward palm smash.

(RTR)

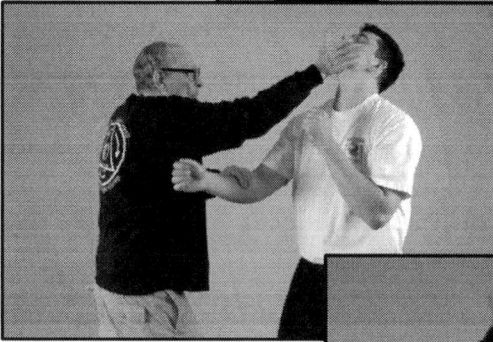

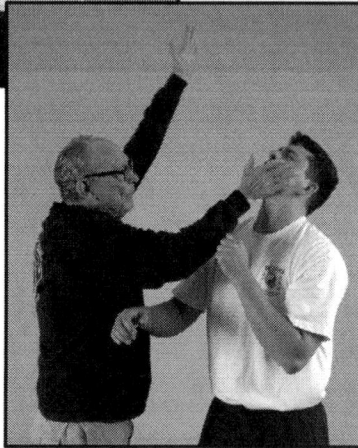

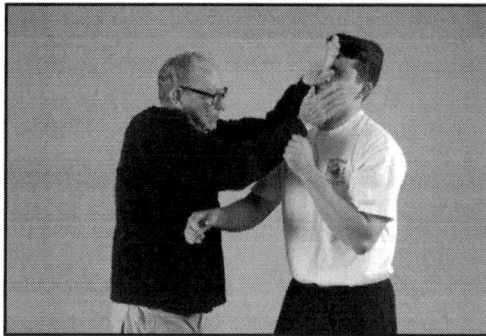

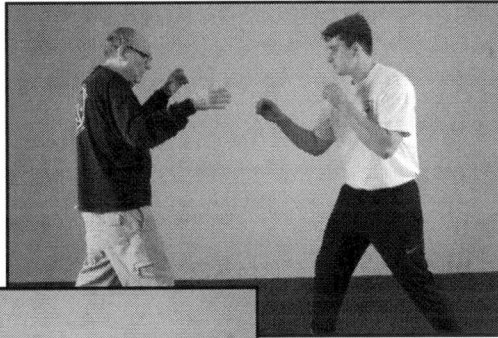

DOUBLE HEAVY
DOWNWARD
PALM SMASH ---
against a take down.

Twist Hand Trap:

Against Straight RT Runch – As your opponent punches you with a straight right blow, you twist your hand with your right palm on top as you hit with a willow leave palm. Stay relaxed as it does not take any strength to parry the hit.

SMALL TIGER MOUTH:

Hit to the throat with an open hand and with the area between your thumb and forefinger.

TAI CHI:

> **Tai Chi Punch** --- staying totally relaxed hit with your rear palm while sinking your weight down as you hit thru his body.

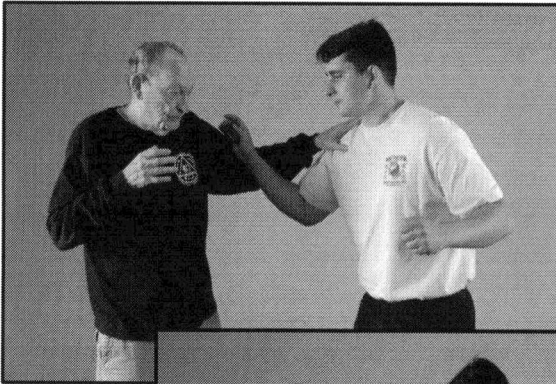

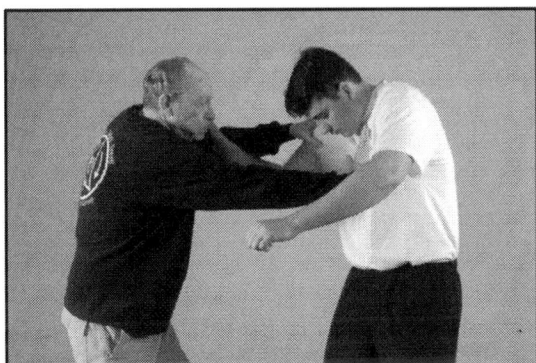

(1) Parry and follow back;

(2) The "follow the hand back" drill --- When your opponent strikes you and you parry it, follow his hand back as it snaps back, trapping his punching hand and pushing him off balance. There are many follow-up possibilities:

Outside parry to follow the hand back to trap:

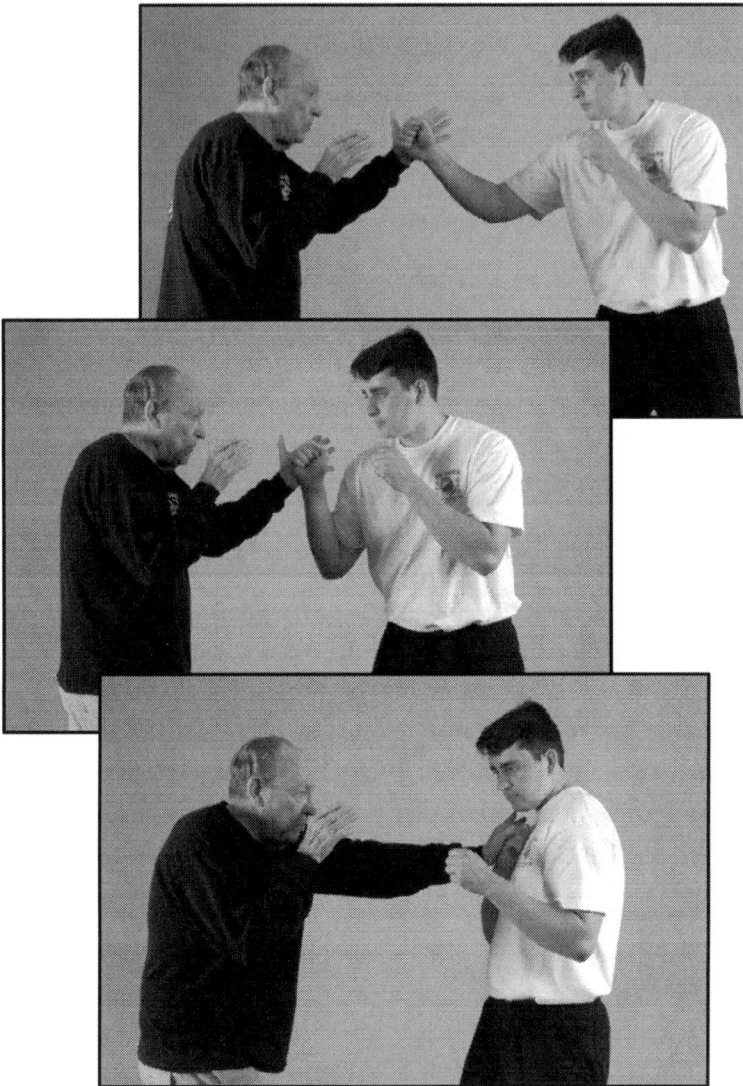

The Lop Sao against straight snap back to trap:

The key to this is when you parry his punch with your rear hand; make sure that your front palm is behind his elbow. This allows you to trap his punch as it snaps back. You then pull him toward you with both arms and finish him with a palm hit.

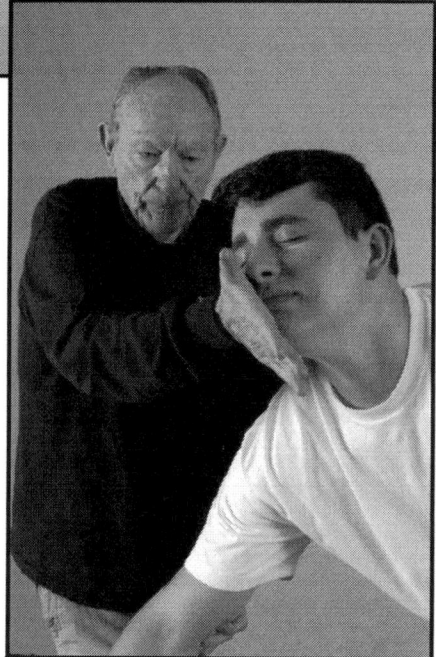

Some Bert Poe:

One of the most important people to add to our growth in Jeet Kune Do was a man who knew absolutely nothing about JKD, but was a warrior with a ton of real world experience. He was married to a high school friend of mine. I met him shortly after I returned home from my Air Force tour in Taiwan. After I opened my kung fu school at the end of 1964, he dropped by to check it out. He was polite, but I realized that he was not impressed. He was a bartender at our local pizza place and I ran in to him a lot and we became friends. As a side note, this place was frequented a lot by our local University of Redlands students. A couple of brothers who went there used it as an idea for a little TV series called *Cheers*.

Around 1974, Bert started showing up at my classes. This was after I starting teaching some of the JKD I was learning from Sifu Dan Inosanto. It turns out that when Bert was teaching boxing at a local gym, one of the boxers started punching and kicking the bag. When asked where he learned to punch and kick like that, Bert was told that it was at my Wednesday night class. When he showed up and watched the class, he told me that it was the first time that he was really impressed with a martial art that also had enough speed and power to destroy an opponent.

Bert's previous combat training consisted of U.S. Marine Corp training Western boxing, real world combat experience, and what techniques he had picked up in various combat hot spots around the world. His basic philosophy to grappling was, "Break something and get back on your feet." Every year that the Smokey Mountain Camp was held, we flew there together. While I taught Jeet Kune Do, he taught what was called *dirty fighting*. Some of that is shown below, but the real dirty stuff has purposely been left out. Some of empty hand combat he taught in my garage is too vicious to share. Below are some of the milder techniques.

407

THE DIVE AGAINST A HAND ATTACK:

Dive forward between his arms. Grab his chin with your fingers in his eyes push his head back. Then shove his lower back as push down hard on his eyes. This should drop him on the back of his head.

THE EYE HIT:

Bert's eye hit is not a finger jab or an eye gouge. It should be used in only in the most extreme circumstances. When your life is in danger. It is very effective to teach a woman as a defense against being raped.

Not a Tiger Claw --- A tiger claw attack is done with the palm cocked back. This does not allow your fingers to penetrate the eyes.

The Poe Eye Hit --- The Poe Eye is done with the tips of the fingers and the fingernails. This attack is meant to destroy the attacker's eyes. You may need to strike at least three times, as hard as you can.

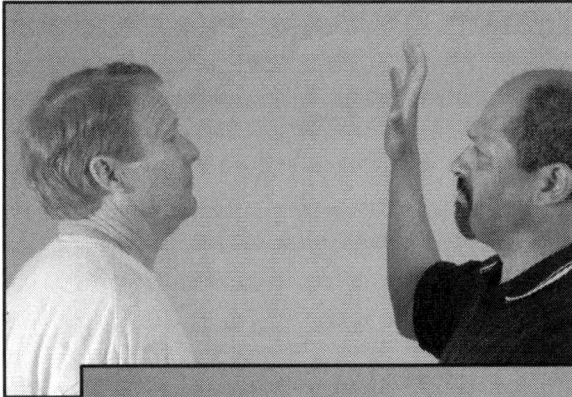

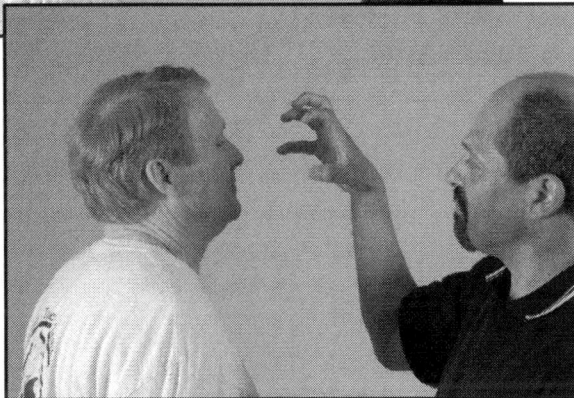

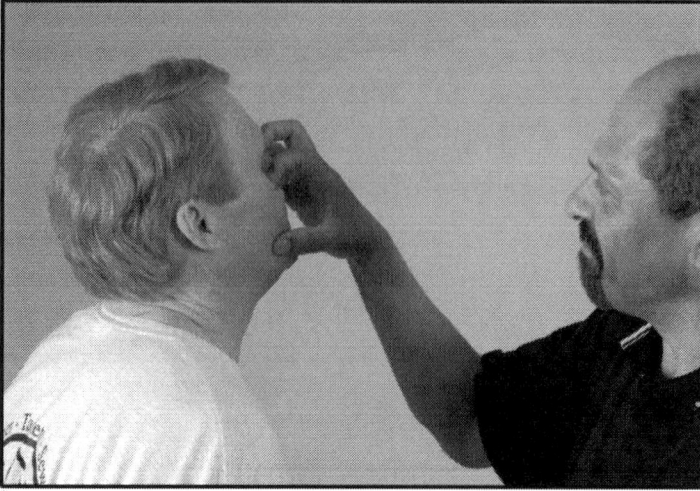

From a 2-Hand Grab --- This is a great technique for women.

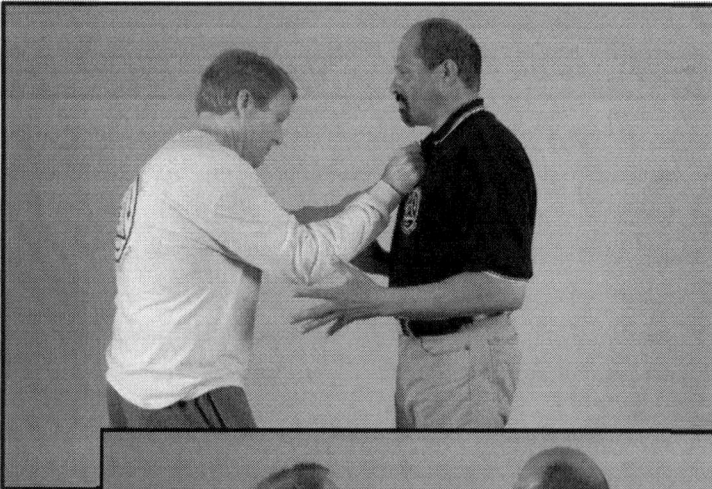

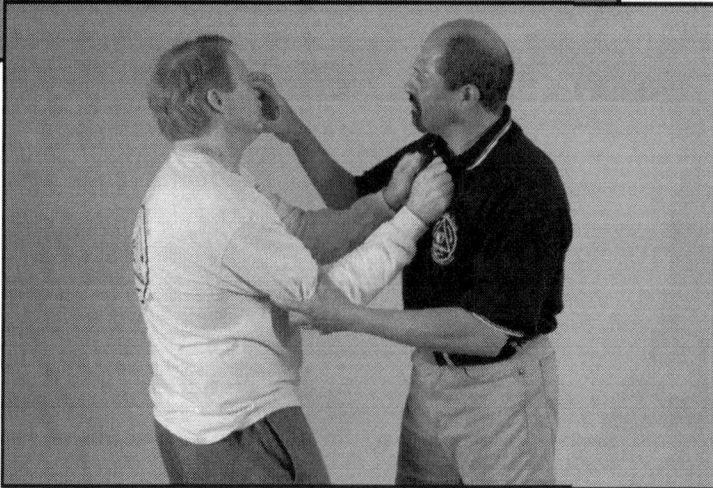

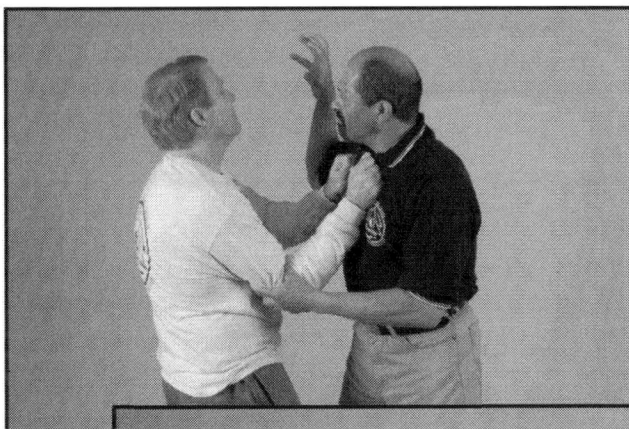

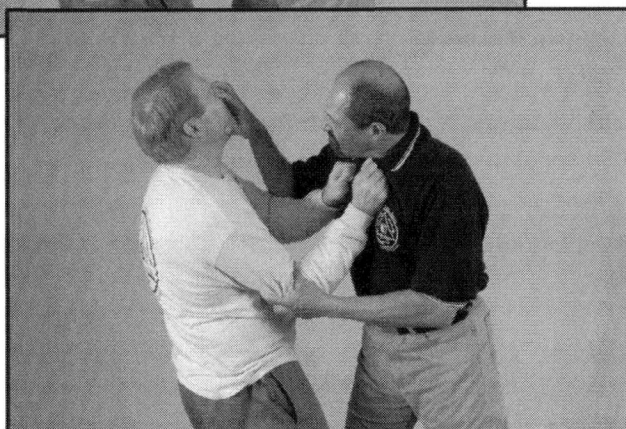

This is done in a series of hits, not just one. It works great when on your back with the opponent on top of you.

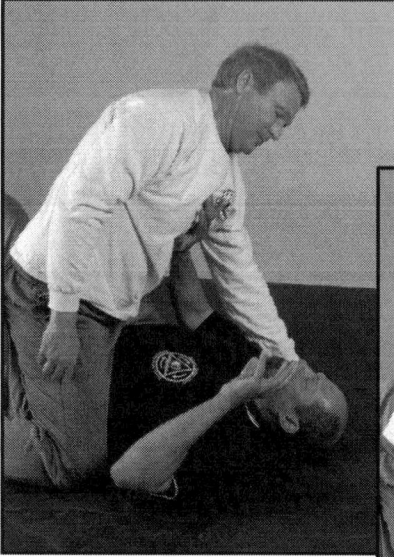

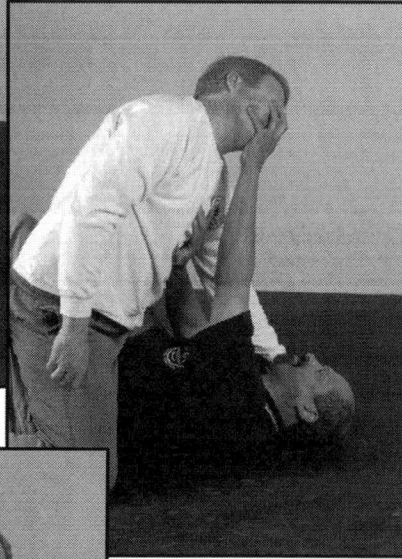

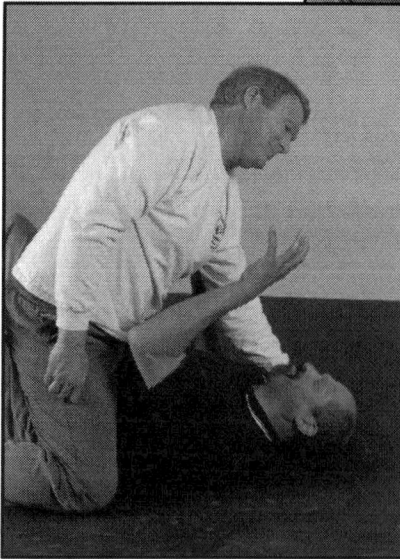

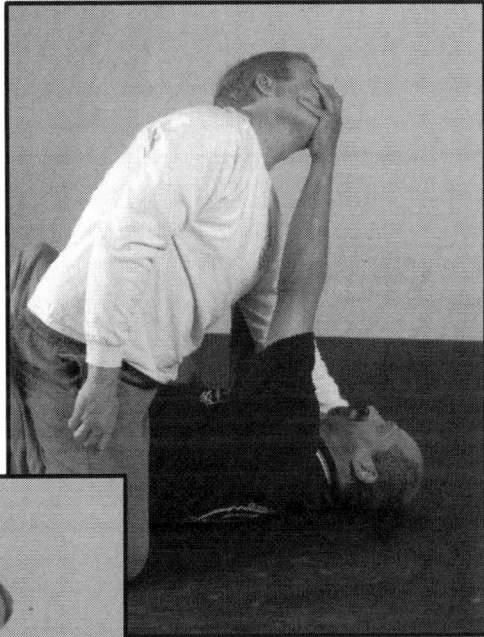

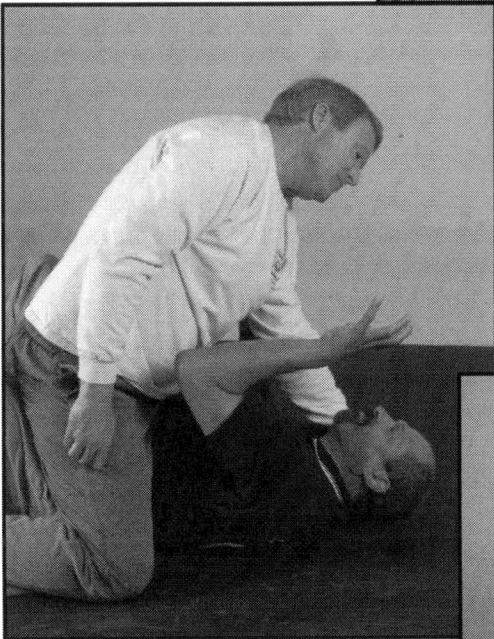

The Face Grab and Turn --- With the tips of your fingers, grab the opponent's face, turn it, and strike the side of his head with a heavy palm strike.

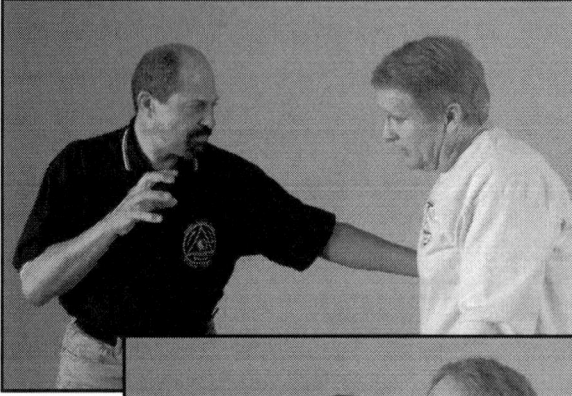

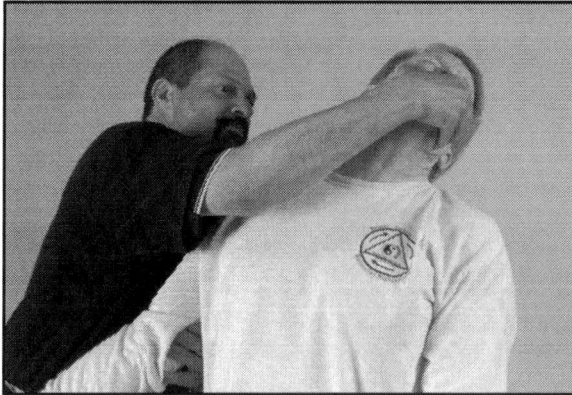

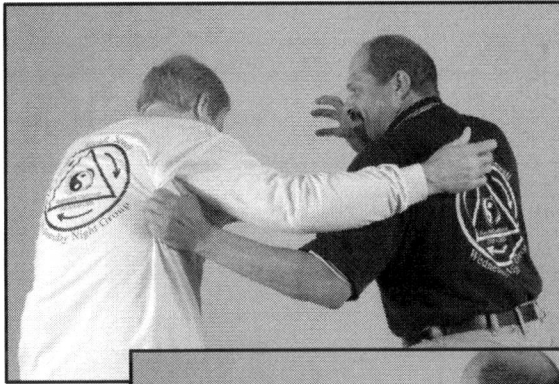

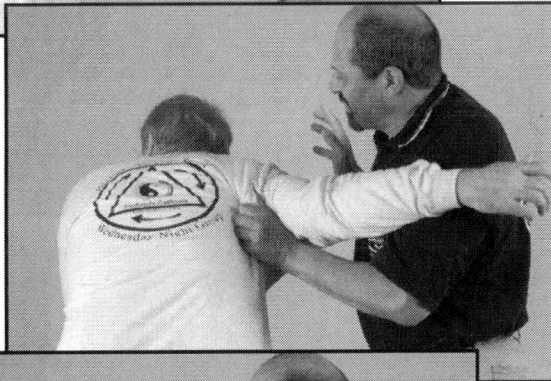

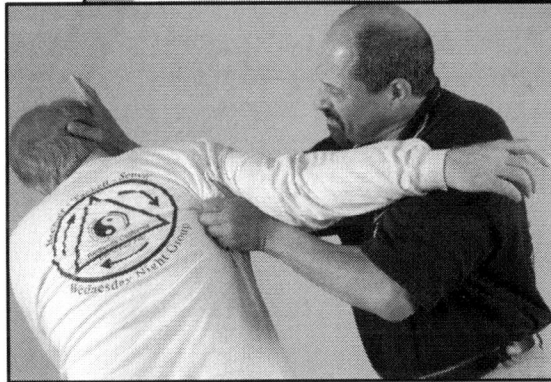

Facing opponent, grab skin and turn him around with you elbow across his back so he cannot elbow you. Then hit him with a heavy palm to his back of his head where the head reaches the neck. Keep hitting until he gets heavy.

415

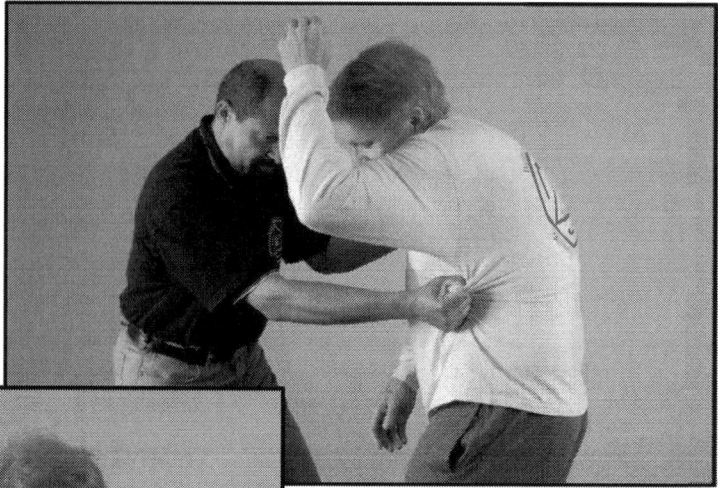

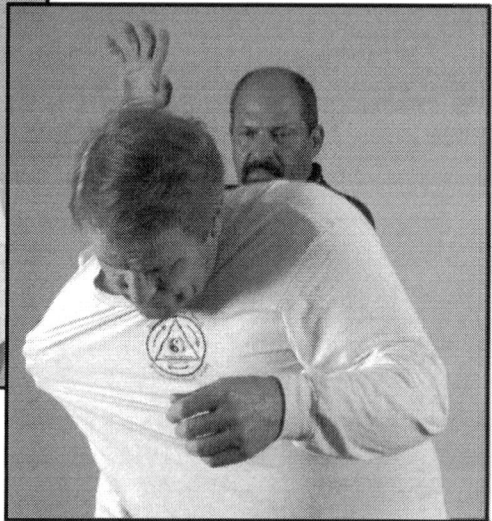

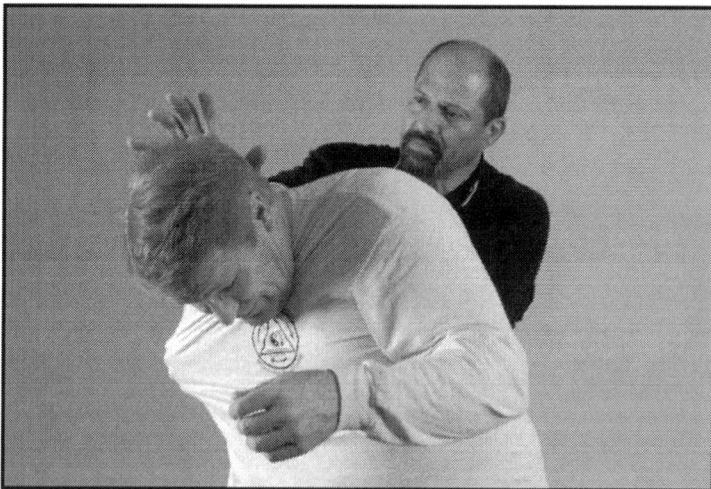

If his back is to you, grab his hair and jerk back. This should cause his mouth to open you then strike his jaw with a palm hook. If his mouth is open, it is easy to break his jaw.

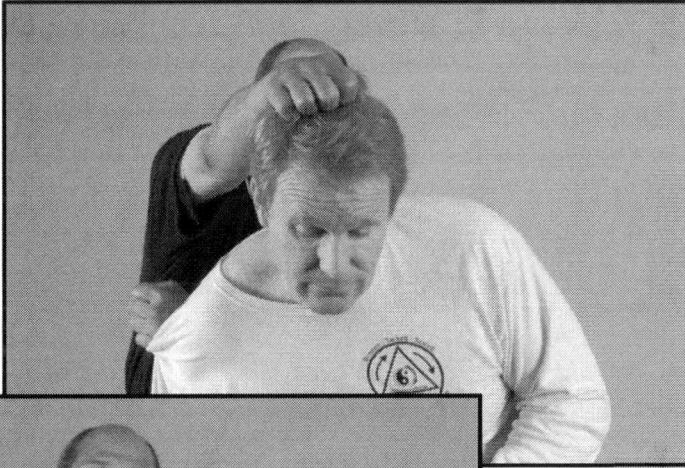

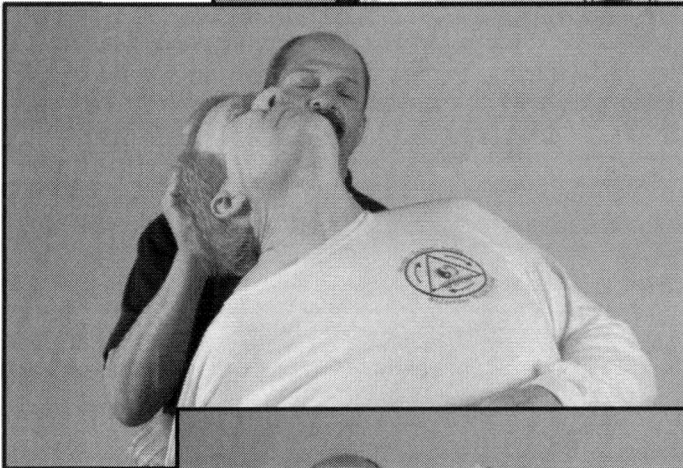

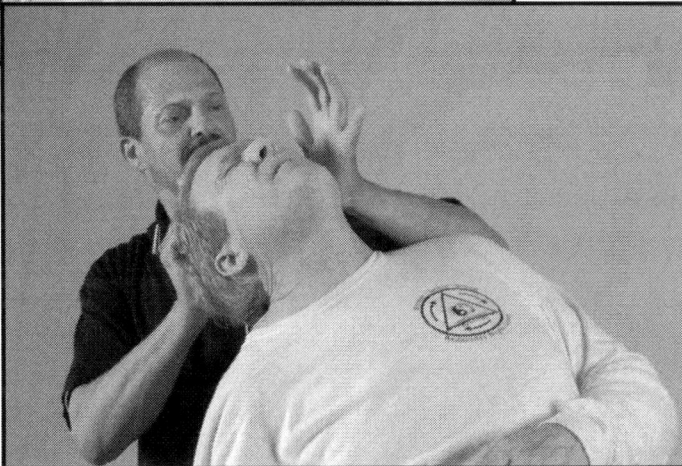

If he has no hair, dig your fingers into his eye sockets by grabbing from behind to jerk his head back, followed by palm hit.

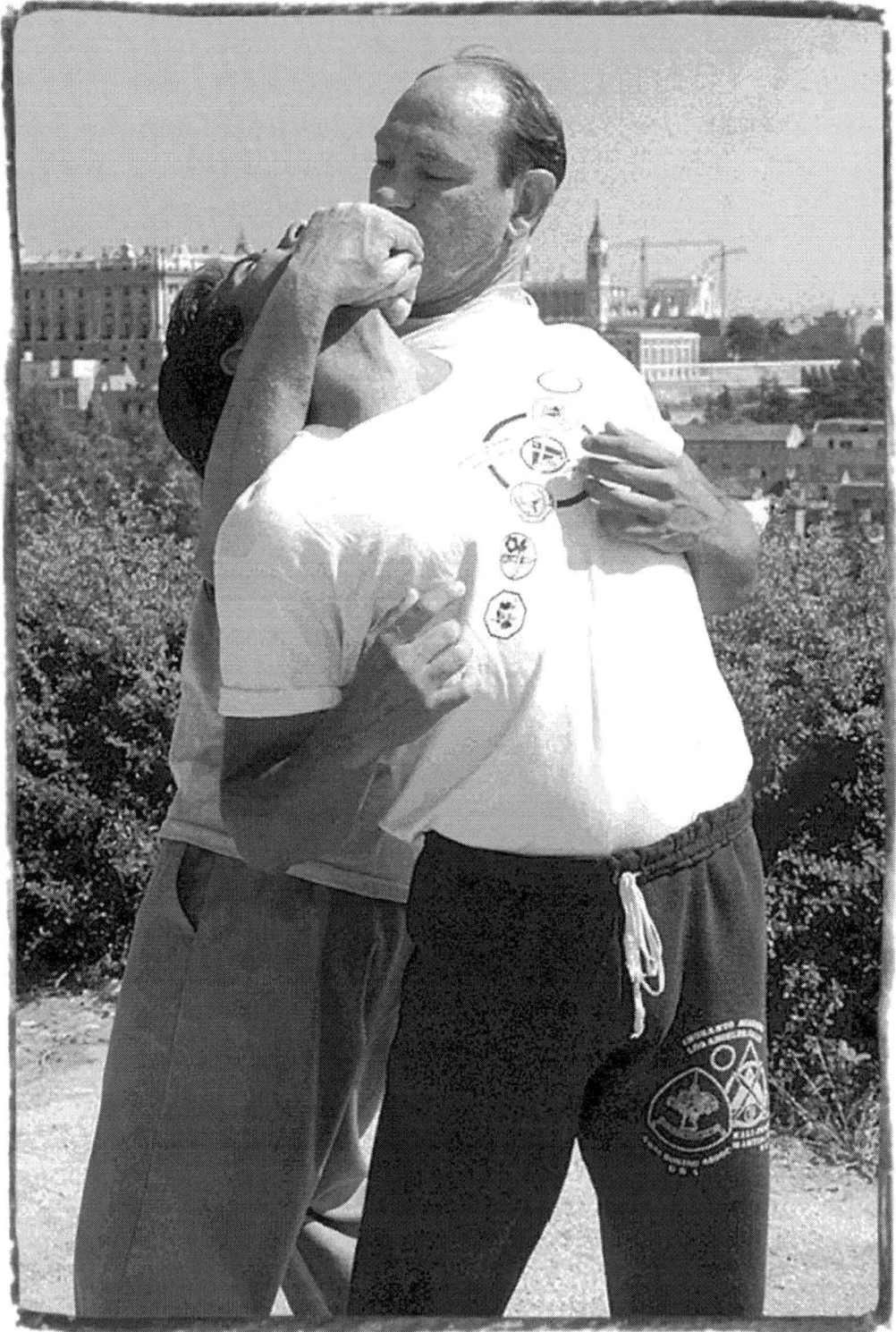

THE DRAGON Story :

If you have read this book, you should be able to understand the meaning of this story --- a fable as told to Bob Bremer by Bruce Lee.

According to Bob Bremer, Bruce Lee was fond of telling stories as way to explain a martial art principle. Bob told the Wednesday Night Group that most of the stories included an old Chinese man of some sort. One of the stories that Bruce told Bob was the story about a woodcutter and a dragon. Bob told us that after Bruce told the story he would just smile and walk away and never mention the story again. He also would never bother to explain the meaning of the story leaving it up to the listener to figure it out. I hope you can understand the meaning. One person having heard Bob tell the story published a version of it in a European martial art magazine. He then tried to explain the meaning of the story, but got the point of it completely wrong. I hope you do better.

Here's the story:

The Woodcutter and the Dragon

ONCE UPON A TIME there was an old Chinese woodcutter. He was very poor. Every day, he went out into the forest hoping to chop enough wood to sell in the town to make enough money to buy rice to feed his family. One day when he was deep in the forest cutting down a tree with his trusty axe, he heard a giant roar from behind on the other side of a clearing. He heard the roar again and saw that the trees were shaking as if there was a huge windstorm. Since the wind was calm where he was, he couldn't figure out what was happening on the other side of the clearing.

He soon found out because a huge dragon suddenly appeared. The woodcutter immediately thought to himself, "If I could kill this dragon, I could sell it for so much money that I could feed my family for the rest of my life and never have to cut wood again". The woodcutter then grabbed his axe and took a step toward the dragon.

The dragon then raised a claw with huge talons on it and said, "Hold it right there you SOB. I know what you want to do. You want to kill me with that axe so you can sell my body for a lot of money. Well, I'm telling you that if you take one more step, I'll blow my fiery breath on you and burn you to a cinder."

The woodcutter figured it was no use to try and kill the dragon so he turned his back on him and went back to chopping the tree down. The second time he went to chop the tree the axe slipped out of his hand and hit the dragon right between the eyes killing him.

End of Story

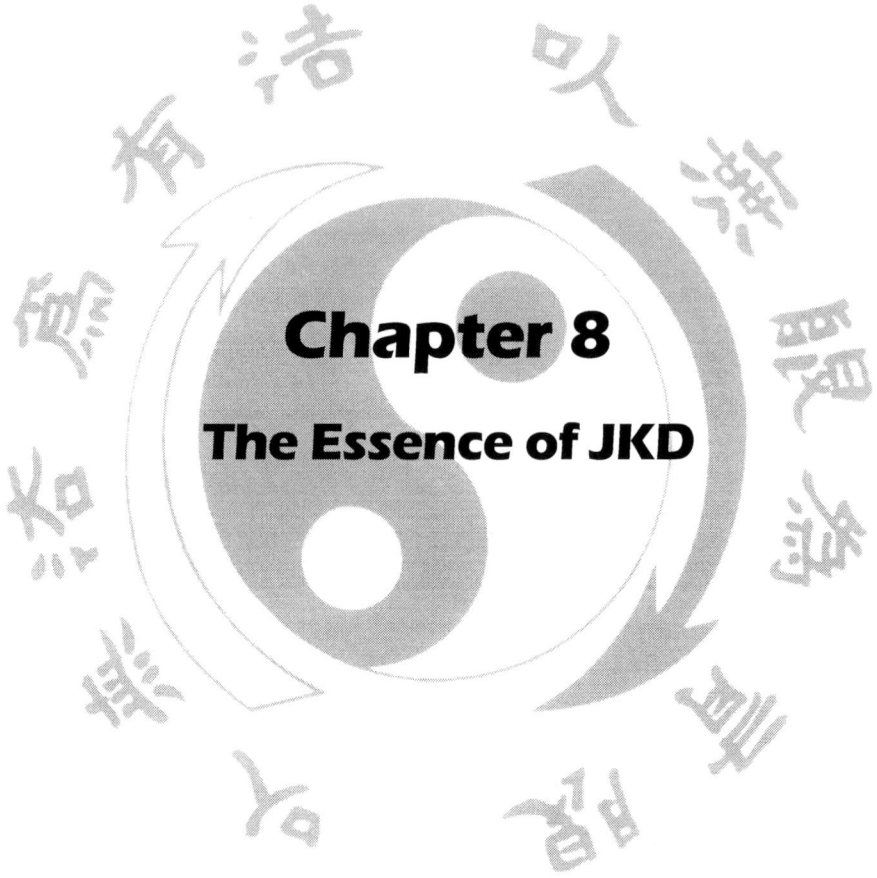

Chapter 8

The Essence of JKD

What is The Essence of JKD?

The goal isn't to try to become a clone of Bruce Lee. Your expression will be colored by your physical attributes and prior training background. Hence, the aim is to train and create your own individual expression by using his "way" as *your way* by using the techniques from this book and your prior training, and finding what works best for you in different circumstances. *Focus on the 80/20% theory.*

If you were paying attention to how many times we used the same basic techniques like the Leg obstruction in many different ways and distances, you should have been able to figure out just what the essence of our JKD is, but don't be bound by any of the techniques shown. Rather train these drills at the different distances shown and put any of the techniques you feel is your essence. Just use this book as a guide to your own discoveries."

The WNG's Essence of JKD --- I think that what we focus on in my garage defines our essence. We try and focus on the following:

-- Basic footwork for attack and defense

-- Power in all tools

-- Intercepting + basic parrying

-- Hammer Principle

-- The leg obstruction

-- Straight lead + basic boxing hands

-- Basic kicks

-- Simplified trapping

-- Controlling distance and rhythm

-- Time commitment theory applied in snapping and heavy hitting

-- Getting rid of the clicks --- i.e., constantly working to become more efficient. I 'm still working on getting it down to mainly just using the finger jab, straight lead and the leg obstruction.

-- Precision and timing

-- Working on basic grappling defense.

-- Daily decrease = working on doing more with less.

While this seems like a long list, you can work a lot of it at the same time. For example, you can work on precision, timing, power, intercepting, and proper distance with the straight lead at the same time by focusing one aspect at a time. To try to do it all at once is a recipe for failure.

The Most Important Aspect of Self Defense: AVOIDING THE FIGHT

The JIM SEWELL story:

ORIGINAL BRUCE LEE STUDENT and fellow Wednesday Night Group teacher, Jim Sewell, has a friend who was just sitting in a bar minding his own business when he looked around he made eye contact with a guy looing of a fight. The guy said, "What's your problem?" It soon escalated into both of them going outside. The guy threw the first punch. Jim's friend blocked it. He then hit the attacker and knocked him down. The only problem was when the guy hit the ground he hit his head on the corner of a concrete planter and died. Even though Jim's friend did not start the fight or threw the first punch, Jim's friend spent six years in prison for manslaughter. The moral of the story is to do whatever you can to avoid the fight. Because of this story, we spend some of our time on how to avoid the fight.

It seems that a lot of fights start in a public situation like a bar. A bar includes men drinking and women. Which is a dangerous combination. The question is how to avoid verbal confrontation that leads to violent confrontation in this environment. It will usually start with a loud question like, *"What the [blank] are you looking at?"* You should learn to practice how to deflect the question. When you deflect his question you redirect his focus with a strip phrase, which is a deflector that strips the phrase of its power.

For example, for the question above you might find something that he is wearing and comment, *"Where did you get that tee shirt? I've been looking for one,"* or you can say that he looks familiar and you think that you might have gone to school with him.

What you are doing is called *Verbal Judo.* I learned a lot of this from Nicholas Hughes at one of his seminars.

Some examples of possible challenging questions and answers are:

Question: *"Are you looking at my girl?"*

Answer: Pretend to recognize her. Come up with an unusual name like Rosalind. Ask him if that is her name. When he says it isn't, tell him that it sure looks like her. Ask *"Is that your girl?"* Tell him that he is a lucky man and offer to buy them both a drink.

Question: *"What's your problem?"*

Possible Answers: *"My wife left me last night,"* or *"I just found out that I have cancer."*

Situation: You bump in to someone accidently. He says, *"Watch where you're going!"*

Your Response: *"Sorry I just got out of the hospital the other day. I had a stroke and don't have all my balance back yet."*

Try to practice these and others in your class every now and then. They may not work all off the time, but it's good to try it anyway. You will not lose anything by trying it. If he does attack you, at least he will look like the jerk he is.

The above ways to diffuse the possible confrontation were taught to me by Nicholas Hughes.

Final Thought: Since Jeet Kune Do means *The Way of the Intercepting Fist,* it is important to be able to intercept with power. To do this efficiently, you must intercept with your strongest hand forward. If you are not doing this, you are just doing kickboxing, which can be very good; but it is not JKD.

The JFD Filter

A JKD Wednesday Night Group Article

By Mike Blesch

BY LABELING JEET KUNE DO as "just a philosophy" with no curriculum or progression of techniques, we rob it of the technical merits of the material taught by its founder, Bruce Lee. On the other hand, by crystallizing the art as "only what Bruce Lee taught," we deprive ourselves of the free expression and naturalness (or perhaps natural-unnaturalness!) advocated so strongly by Bruce Lee.

Our group does not believe that either approach is wholly correct. The Original JKD material combined with the philosophical elements contained within Bruce Lee's notes and writings provide a foundation upon which we build our own personal martial art. In our case, this is the origin of *Old-School JKD.*

Using the principles laid out by Bruce Lee, along with an understanding of the foundation and *function* of Jeet Kune Do, we can investigate other arts and draw out their essence. We call this the *JKD Filter.*

Jack-Of-All-Trades or Master of Some?

Many will say that the only way to be a true martial artist is to train *everything*: Boxing, Wrestling, Jiu-Jitsu, and Judo for competition. Kali for weapons, Reality-based martial arts for self-defense, and so on. All have been pressure tested and proven effective. No doubt. However, there are two significant questions that I feel every martial artist who cross-trains in this manner should ask himself:

> *(1) Is it more efficient to flow from one art to another (and one delivery system to another) than to have a single platform from which I can utilize all of my attacks and defenses?*

426

(2) Does an accumulation of techniques make me a better fighter or would I benefit from limiting the amount of tools I train in order to hone each one to a very high level?

Time is every human beings most valuable asset. When taking into account that fighting arts like Boxing, Wrestling, or JKD require athletic ability, which often begins to disappear as we reach middle age, efficient use of training time becomes critical. This is one of the reasons why daily decrease is such an important JKD principle. How can I perform the required repetitions to "master" any given technique if I'm spending my training time adding new techniques or practicing many different arts using different structures?

Applying the JKD Filter

We are always looking for a better way, trying to find more efficient tools and examining our own weaknesses. Constant research and experimentation are necessary. However, in order to get maximum benefit from our training time we must have some way of filtering a vast amount of material without having to train *everything*. In simple terms, this is how we analyze new material:

Necessity --- *Does it add something that is lacking from our game?*

Structure --- *Do we have to change our delivery system to accommodate the new technique or does it fit in with what we're already doing?*

A basic example of this would be a technique which doesn't work well from an unmatched stance (i.e. Right lead vs left lead) forcing us to change leads in order to use it and thereby negating the advantage of the dominant side forward structure and telegraphing our intent.

Adaptability --- *How limited is its application?* Will it work against different types of fighters? Against different methods of defense? Under less than ideal conditions?

Vulnerability --- *Does it leave us exposed to counterattacks, which may be more damaging than the initial attack we're defending against?*

"It's not what you can learn, it's what you can throw away."
--- BRUCE LEE *(to Bob Bremer)*

It's not important for us to tell you what you should to throw away or what you should add. This must come from your own study and experience. What we can give you is a way to help you decide.

**"Spend 80% of your time
on what you will use 80% of the time."**

--- TIM TACKETT

The 80/20 Rule:

Also known as the *Pareto Principle,* the 80/20 rule states that quite often 80% of your results will come from 20% of your efforts. Therefore, to achieve maximum results, you should spend 80% of your time on the 20% that matters. This is a very useful idea, which has been applied successfully to numerous disciplines. For our group, it essentially functions as a ***Second level to the JKD Filter*** by reminding us to focus on the core techniques and principles of JKD. The trick is figuring out exactly which techniques make up the vital 20% that will deliver 80% of the results.

When it comes to combat sports like MMA and boxing, the task is somewhat simpler because of the detailed statistics available. We can discern that for a lightweight MMA fighter more fights are finished by submission than KO, so the fighters training habits need to reflect that. The opposite becomes true for the Welterweight class and above. Admittedly, there is more than one way to interpret the data (i.e. smaller fighters need to work on their punching power and larger fighters need to work on their submissions), but that isn't relevant to the current discussion.

In boxing, we find that the fighter that throws the most jabs usually wins. The trouble with a "street fighting" art like Jeet Kune Do is that there is no accurate way to obtain those types of statistics.

Then how do we decide which techniques will be our primary responses *(the vital 20%)*? The solution for us has been threefold:

(1) **Following JKD principles** – Particularly *economy of motion;*

(2) **Individualization** – Accounting for strengths, weaknesses and temperament; and,

(3) **Testing** – Learning from successes and failures in sparring and scenario training, as well as in the ring/cage.

NOTES

NOTES

NOTES

27853691R00255

Printed in Great Britain
by Amazon